Watercourses in the Community

A guide to sustainable watercourse
management in the urban environment

June 2000

THE INSTITUTION OF
CIVIL ENGINEERS

THE CITY OF EDINBURGH COUNCIL

Scottish
WILDLIFE TRUST

SCOTTISH
NATURAL
HERITAGE

Promoting Scottish Local Government

WWF

SCOTTISH
BIODIVERSITY
GROUP

Urban Design Alliance

Chairman's Foreword

The Scottish Environment Protection Agency (SEPA) aims 'to promote the conservation and enhancement of the natural beauty and amenity of controlled waters and the conservation of flora and fauna dependent on aquatic environments'.

Historically, environmental improvements have been secured by SEPA through regulation, but new initiatives and new partnerships with external organisations are enabling more non-statutory opportunities for encouraging environmental gain. With the launch of the Habitat Enhancement Initiative (HEI) in July 1998 such opportunities are extending to habitat and conservation issues.

For SEPA to maximise these opportunities a range of resources has been developed through HEI, which provide guidance on good management practice for aquatic habitats. This document, *Watercourses in the Community*, is the second in a series of documents to be produced to provide, to both internal and external staff, simple clear guidelines for the management of Scotland's urban rivers.

'Watercourses in the Community' has been produced in partnership with key environmental organisations in Scotland, in association with the Institution of Civil Engineers, for whose contribution SEPA is extremely grateful. The document has been developed over the past two years through workshops and task groups and SEPA would like to take this opportunity to thank all those who have contributed to the production of *Watercourses in the Community,* especially the local authorities whose input has been invaluable.

In Scotland, many of our urban rivers and streams have been constrained, degraded and hidden beneath concrete. Take the opportunity to learn from this working document how you can help to protect and enhance these important Scottish habitats.

Ken Collins
Chairman, Scottish Environment Protection Agency

Index

Habitat Enhancement

Scottish Environment Protection Agency

Going against the flow

Follow the path upstream and work towards the future...

Manage it

Maintain it

Monitor it

Enforce it

Implement it

Find the funding

Agree a scheme

Agree a Plan

What are the problems - What are the options?
Undertake a watercourse survey to find out what is there, think about different courses of action and the associated problems.

What do People Want?
Find out how the residents would like their neighbourhood to look and to function. - Pre consultation.

Recognise the Importance
Urban watercourses offer small opportunities, but there are many of them. Cumulatively they amount to a big lost opportunity to enhance quality of life, increase biodiversity, help reverse the decline of urban areas, reduce development in the countryside, reduce dependence on car use, energy consumption, air pollution, and global warming.

The World of Scottish

Opportunities for the Built Environment

Water can provide fine settings for many buildings - from intimate settings around small burns, to grand vistas across major rivers. Ideals:
- make the most of water-frontages
- use SUDS in all developments to minimise run-off, often they enhance the surroundings
- maximise the quality of the design

See chapters 2, 3, 4 & 5

Working with Water

Catchments

Watercourses, drainage, and flooding are natural systems which naturally establish an equilibrium. Human interference often causes problems:
- increasing run-off = flooding
- straightening rivers = increased erosion
- building on floodplains = increased flooding downstream

Wherever possible natural river systems should remain untouched; if it is necessary to interfere, every effort should be made to maintain the natural balance

See chapter 4

Sustainable Urban Drainage Systems (SUDS)

SUDS are techniques which encourage rainwater to drain into the soil, or slow-draining channels and ponds - as opposed to fast draining pipes leading directly into watercourses.

The use of SUDS:
- reduces the downstream flow
- reduces the power of the water
- reduces the risk of flooding
- helps maintain flows in periods of dry weather
- improves water quality downstream
- increases amenity value.

Soft Engineering & Sustainability
- natural process and materials
- use modeling techniques to predict effects
- unsustainable practice has cost millions, eg in 1994 West Central Scotland floods cost £100,000,000 in damage

See chapter 4

Consultation & Community

It is important that community involvement is encouraged - for both short term and long term benefit. There is a lot of help and advice available - this booklet for instance! All involved parties should be heard and clear objectives outlined.

See chapters 5 & 6

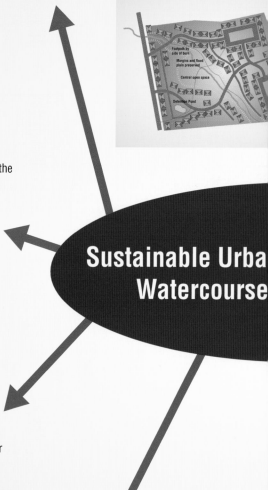

Sustainable Urba
Watercourse

Restoration

Many urban watercourses are buried in pipes, channelled in concrete, or concealed behind flood defence banks. Few play a positive part in our towns - either for people or nature. This will hopefully become a thing of the past. Ideals:
- Best Value: don't adhere to traditional practices - work with nature
- eliminate safety hazards not public access
- work towards the best long-term outcome
- be realistic - achieve your goals
- benefit all - the environment, the economy and the community

See chapters 3 & 4

See chapter 5 for step by step guide on river restoration

Rivers and Burns

Opportunities for People

The UK aims to:
- increase the population living in urban areas
- reduce development pressures on the countryside

The Key is improving the quality of life in urban areas... and urban watercourses can help, through providing:
- areas of natural beauty and places of tranquility
- leisure and recreation
- cycling and pedestrian routes
- access to green space
- opportunities for fishing

See chapters 2, 4 & 5

Opportunities for Nature

The UK aims to protect and enhance wildlife, through designations and protective measures, implemented at both national and local level, eg Biodiversity Action Plans.

Watercourses:
- support a vast range of species in and outside the water
- are keys to increasing biodiversity

Urban watercourses:
- are the richest natural habitats in the town
- important wildlife corridors

A bad stretch can endanger wildlife, and the influence can be felt for many miles..

Watercourses should provide:
- pollution free water
- free passage for wildlife up and down the river
- decent, natural habitats in and around the water, such as meanders, pools, riffles and gravel beds, bankside vegetation
- natural features
- areas that are free from disturbance

Remember - action in one part of the river will cause a reaction elsewhere!

See chapters 2, 4 & 5

Policy, Law & Regulation

There are many different regulations in force from EU level downwards. They are intended to:
- prevent damage to habitats
- prevent damage to species
- prevent works that could cause flooding
- ensure the safety of the public

See chapters 4 & 7

Organisations and Responsibilities
- Who is in charge of watercourses?
- Who is in charge of habitats and nature conservation?
- Who do I need to ask if I want to do anything to a watercourse?
- Where can I volunteer?

See chapters 5, 6 & 7

Planning

Planning policies exist at national and local level to:
- prevent development in areas which are prone to flooding
- protect existing watercourses and habitats
- require the use of sustainable urban drainage techniques

Many local authorities will be adopting the recommendations in this guidance for the protection and positive use of watercourses.

See chapter 6

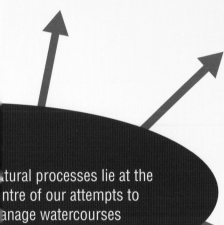

tural processes lie at the ntre of our attempts to anage watercourses

Funding

Many schemes to restore watercourses, r to introduce sustainable urban drainage ystems (SUDS) will pay for hemselves - benefits...
- attract people
- can increase the value of property next to the watercourse (up to 20%)
- help support tourism which is a major employer

UDS are..
- normally cheaper to maintain
- help to reduce flooding and the need for expensive flood protection measures

ut these measures require money up-front. here are two approaches worth trying:
- apply for funding specifically to restore a watercourse
- apply for funding for a large project of which the restoration of the watercourse is a part, eg the creation of a riverside cycle route under the Local Transport Plan

ee chapter 5

Flooding can cause extensive damage to property and misery to the owners. © *G Burns, SCP*

"Development of an area which is exposed to frequent or extensive flooding is likely to be unsustainable and should be avoided. Where development is essential the threat of flooding should be managed in an environmentally sensitive way. The role of soft engineering measures such as natural flood meadows and washlands in attenuating flooding should be recognised, and additional flood protection measures should only be adopted after consideration of all available techniques which can provide the appropriate level of protection...." National Planning Policy Guidance 7 gives clear guidance (NPPG 7 1995).

Introduction

This report has been produced as part of the Scottish Environment Protection Agency's Habitat Enhancement Initiative. It considers both the benefits that can be obtained from the sensitive management of our urban watercourses, and the harm done by neglecting them.

It has been produced in partnership with a wide range of organisations including the Urban Design Alliance, a group of institutions involved in the management of urban areas. The formation of this partnership reflects:
- the growing consensus that we should act to improve the quality of our towns and cities in the overall interests of sustainable development, and secondly;
- the need for professionals to work together.

Surveys show that about half of the UK population want to live in the countryside, reflecting the fact that many people are dissatisfied with the quality of life in urban areas. Urban lifestyles can have a smaller impact on the environment than car-dependent rural

Perth and the River Tay
© *Paul Tompkins/S.T.B./Still Moving Picture Company*

lifestyles. Much thought is being given to ways of attracting people to live in urban areas. The quality of the environment is a key factor, and what better way is there of providing an urban environment of superb quality than through the watercourses that run through it?

This is not an aspirational report - it is a practical one. It promotes the wise use of money as well the improvement of the environment in which we live.
- The engineering techniques advocated have been proven internationally as cost-effective, safe and practicable.
- The commercial value of using watercourses as an enhancement to development has been demonstrated by examples in the UK and world-wide.
- The internationally recognised goal of sustainable development, to which this document intends to make a contribution, is mainstream policy of all political parties.

"In the past, 'improving' rivers often meant increasing their flow capacity. In future, it should refer to multi-purpose schemes designed to improve the capacity of each river valley to function as a visual amenity, a recreation area, a fishery, a nature reserve, a water supply, a storm detention area, a drainage network, and a movement corridor for boats, walkers, cyclists and equestrians"

Tom Turner, Landscape Planning 1987

If when you are reading this guide there are terms or acronyms you don't recognise, check the glossary at the back.

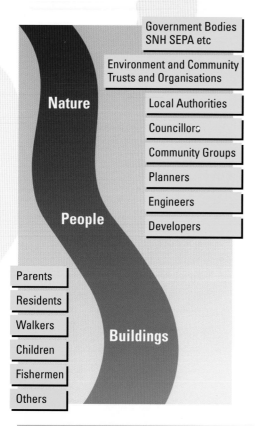

Government Bodies
SNH SEPA etc

Environment and Community
Trusts and Organisations

Local Authorities

Councillors

Community Groups

Planners

Engineers

Developers

Nature

People

Buildings

Parents

Residents

Walkers

Children

Fishermen

Others

Who is this report for?

This report is aimed at anyone who is involved in the development and management of urban areas, from drainage through to architecture.

What is the report's purpose? - Sustainability

The report covers an important element of sustainable development and Agenda 21. It shows how watercourses can contribute to increased biodiversity, enhance urban areas, increase profits from development, and improve conditions for people who live in urban areas.

It outlines current techniques, philosophy and legislation regarding the sustainable management and engineering of watercourses and where to go to obtain further information and advice.

The guide hopes to convince people of the importance of taking urban watercourses seriously, and to encourage them to find the advice, reference documents, guidance, and funding which will enable them to get on with the job: the restoration, protection & appreciation of Scotland's urban burns and rivers.

Four Paths to Sustainability

Economic
Development

Social
Progress

Sustainable
Development

Conservation
of Resources

Protection of
the Environment

- **social progress** - by improving the attractiveness and quality of life of existing communities;
- **protection of the environment** - by reversing the decline in natural habitats and biodiversity in urban areas;
- **conservation of resources** - by encouraging new development in urban areas which meet people's needs without the need for extensive car use, and provide an alternative to development on greenfield sites and in the countryside;
- **economic development** - by increasing the profitability of development and reducing the costs of drainage and the damage caused by flooding.

1. The Importance of Urban Watercourses

Burns and rivers - beauty, richness - and a powerful force in the landscape

The Scottish landscape has developed over tens of thousands of years, and water has played a major role: eroding rocks and soil, and moving and depositing silt, sand and gravel. A rich variety of plants and animals has evolved in these conditions. A natural river, the land through which it flows and the life it supports are intertwined. There are many different types of river but some of the most common features are:

- pools and riffles - in many natural watercourses a chain forms, linking pools of slow flowing water with fast flowing riffles. The riffles increase the oxygen levels in the water. Both offer different habitats for fish and other wildlife.
- gravel beds - a natural watercourse carries substantial quantities of gravel and sediment. The gravel beds provide an important wildlife habitat and are essential breeding grounds for many fish.
- meanders - develop where the watercourse is gently descending.
- floodplain - an area of land which floods when flows are high. The flood plain stores water and sediment, which reduces peak flows downstream.
- bankside vegetation - trees naturally reinforce the banks and reduce the rate of erosion. The leaves add to the food supply and provide shade, which helps keep the water cool in summer and reduces excessive growth of vegetation in the water.

A typical urban watercourse

Ours is often a legacy of buried watercourses, concrete culverts, environmental damage and uncompromising ugliness. We also have significant amounts of development in areas which flood. But there is great potential to make good.

Common features of urban watercourses

Often of little value to nature

- concrete and steel lined channels and culverts, outfalls and flap-valves surrounded with concrete, banks protected with concrete and steel;
- artificially straightened channels - no meanders, pools or riffles;
- high flood embankments;
- mechanically excavated channels - with steep, sparsely vegetated banks;

Often of little value to people

- cut off from the life of the town, hidden behind fences and walls, buried in pipes, with no public access. Most urban development excludes watercourses, placing them at the back of buildings and gardens. There is an "out-of-sight out-of-mind" mentality which regards watercourses as a safety hazard and an inconvenience.
- marred by refuse and litter - including large items such as shopping trolleys.

Watercourses are dynamic by nature - they vary from slow meandering streams to bubbling rapids.
Upper Spey © P A Mcdonald

Shee Water, Glenshee. © *George Logan*

Most urban watercourses play no part in the life of the town. They benefit neither people nor nature. It is the smaller rivers and burns that have been lost or degraded to the greatest extent. ©*RPH Ravensbourne*

GARDY-LOO. While people were dying in epidemics the preservation of natural habitats was of secondary importance. Watercourses were considered part of the problem.

Watercourse or sewer? - or both?
A typical urban stream with culverting and associated cross connection problems. *Edinburgh © SEPA*

Many watercourses have been modified with one objective in mind - the unimpeded movement of water. They offer little for people or wildlife. Some have been lined with concrete to cope with the increased storm flows caused by urbanisation. *© RPH*

How is it we have ignored our urban watercourses?

The water environment has been so important to the development of our towns and cities, with uses ranging from drinking and a source of food, to transport and power. It seems incredible that it plays so small a part today. But there are good reasons.

Early days of drainage

Right from the earliest days of the development of towns, watercourses were used as sewers. Once used in that way, there was never any reason to incorporate them positively into the town. The Victorians believed that sewage gas odours spread infectious and fatal diseases. Many watercourses were subsequently buried in pipes. While the Victorians clearly valued nature, and created many of today's urban parks, the industrial revolution was largely at the expense of the natural environment. The main effort was directed at the alleviation of poverty, malnutrition and epidemics rather than the general protection of the environment.

To increase drainage both of agricultural land and of towns, burns and rivers were often straightened and deepened. The faster flows of water broke the natural equilibrium of the watercourses and increased erosion and the transfer of gravels and sediments. Downstream this brought problems of increased flooding and sediment deposition. Having interfered once, ongoing maintenance would then be necessary to prevent the clogging of channels and erosion of banks. New flood embankments would be needed downstream to cope with the increased flows. The Victorians had no science of catchment management, nor understanding of hydraulics, hydrology and geomorphology. People were unable to foresee the consequences of large-scale changes to the drainage of a river catchment.

There were no administrative structures in place able to manage water over a wide catchment. Flooding problems were dealt with at a local level, mostly by building up flood banks and by straightening rivers, transferring the problem downstream. Also, towns were being developed and managed independently of the management of watercourses, so the exclusion of urban watercourses from towns was a bureaucratic inevitability.

Growing Towns - the pressure of development

Through the 19th and 20th centuries urban streets were being progressively re-surfaced with waterproof concrete and tarmac and greenfields were being replaced with buildings, so rain which would once have slowly drained off or filtered into the soil, would, instead, drain rapidly into watercourses by a direct network of pipes. Again, the same combination of increased storm flows and new flooding problems arose resulting in the same answer: to build up flood protection banks, straighten meanders, and replace natural channels with concrete.

Hungry for land, towns sometimes expanded into natural floodplains. "Living memory" failed to warn against development in areas prone to flooding; and when the development did flood, there would be strong pressure for flood protection works. These embankments, while tackling the local problem, blocked off the floodplains that had previously absorbed flood waters, causing more water to be channelled downstream, and with it, the danger of flooding elsewhere.

Developers found it easier to put watercourses into underground culverts and then overlay a standard road layout, rather than "work" the development in around the watercourse. The consequence has been developments which are structured for convenience rather than natural beauty, and are impossible to tell apart.

We are increasingly being left with a network of buried watercourses which do nothing to enrich the communities through which they flow.

Development on natural flood plains inevitably leads to flooded buildings, unless flood embankments and pumping stations are provided.
Flooding near factory, Elgin © A R Black

Safety concerns

Safety concerns were dealt with by excluding people rather than eliminating the hazard. Safety improvements invariably meant fencing-off the watercourse or putting it underground in a culvert, rather than introducing measures to make the watercourse inherently safer. Such measures work so long as they keep people out. But agile children can climb most types of fencing and, unless regularly maintained and inspected, fencing can become broken down. People are kept out of culverts by heavy grills at either end. These grills can collect debris and become blocked, contributing to the flood hazard. There have also been examples of youngsters launching determined attacks on grills to open the culvert to exploration. To resist attack, grills have to be heavy and expensive.

Rather than incorporate watercourses into the life of a town, the traditional option has been to bury them in culverts. © A Church, SEPA

And so...

Having started with burns and rivers that were attractive to people, full of life, and cost nothing to maintain, we have developed a system of underground drains, reinforced river banks, flood protection schemes, pumping stations, concrete channels, grills and fences, which is an ongoing cost to the community and provides, at best, a single benefit and, at worst, causes problems.

There can be no question of blaming past generations who acted in good faith on the knowledge available then. But perhaps we should blame ourselves if we continue in the traditional ways, when engineering and science now offer far more effective, economical, and sustainable alternatives.

Traditionally we have tried to deal with safety by removing public access, rather than removing the hazards. © SEPA

New techniques to work in harmony with nature

We now have a better understanding of the complexity of river systems and an appreciation of the importance of the natural environment. This better understanding of how rivers work has brought engineering techniques which work with nature rather than fight against it. These techniques can be employed in a natural way and are often invisible. There are two main classes:

Soft engineering - using natural processes to do the work for us
- banks protected with natural materials or vegetation;
- siphon outlets used instead of conventional piped outlets;
- the natural engineering techniques make watercourses safer;
- soft engineering can also be used to create natural habitats.

Sustainable Urban Drainage Systems

These aim to address the problems of flooding by tackling them at source
- rainfall is dealt with by percolation through the soil and temporary storage, rather than by piped drains, allowing contaminants to be intercepted and pollution in adjacent watercourses reduced;
- networks of detention and retention ponds and wetlands can be created which filter out pollutants and add to the amenity value for the community.

There is now a great opportunity to enhance the watercourses in urban areas.

Watercourses can and should be an attractive part of the urban environment, yet it is unsustainable to continue to build on the floodplain.
Leithan Water © SEPA

2. Opportunities with urban watercourses

In essence...

Soft engineering, sustainable urban drainage systems and our better understanding of catchments and the forces of nature mean that we now have a great opportunity to restore the burns and rivers that run through our towns and cities.

Opportunities for nature

Urban stretches of burns and rivers do not need to provide a poor habitat or act as a barrier to the movement of wildlife up and downstream; a natural watercourse running through a town can support hundreds of different species, both below and above water and in the surrounding margins. They also provide an important passageway for wildlife. Why not:

- establish a continuous natural habitat both in the watercourse itself and along the banks - right through the urban area
- introduce measures which will protect the watercourse from pollution
- restore the watercourse to a more natural form

A healthy watercourse can support a wide range of wildlife. This is a large backwater formed by a sensitive river restoration scheme. © *RRC*

Opportunities for people

Many of those towns and cities that have cherished their watercourses now reap their advantage as tourist attractions. Tourism is one of Scotland's major industries. In Glasgow, Edinburgh and Inverness (to name just three of Scotland's towns), the main rivers are still valued parts of the town, but many smaller watercourses are lost.

Watercourses can be the most attractive feature in an urban area, and a place of real beauty. They act as a magnet to both adults and children. Watercourses can be used to provide new pedestrian or cycle walks, places to sit by, to enjoy, for play, for fishing, for education and so on. Watercourses may provide the only access to open space for urban dwellers. Restoring the water to a more natural appearance is vital and may:

- provide access for humans;
- provide amenity areas, such as dipping platforms, seating, sheltered areas;
- therefore use watercourses to provide new, safe and attractive routes for pedestrians and cyclists.

Water is a magnet for people of all ages. Good design plus stewardship can significantly reduce safety hazards. © *RPH*

Opportunities for the built environment

Watercourses can provide a delightful setting for buildings, which can be reflected in the price and the profits of development. Better knowledge of which areas flood means that development on land that floods can be avoided.

The latest engineering techniques can reduce flooding, and help tackle pollution by:

- ensuring new development takes full advantage of the presence of water;
- in existing developments, reintroducing watercourses as a focus;
- introducing measures which will prevent or dissipate storm flows and flooding.

Development on a river's natural flood plain, may often lead to retrospective and costly flood defence works. Perth and the River Tay. © *Paul Tompkins/S.T.B./Still Moving Picture Company*

Otter. © Laurie Campbell, SNH

This swale will help prevent oil and heavy metals from the road from entering the river system. © SEPA

A 'porous' road surface helps to reduce run-off and pollution. © SEPA

8

WATER VOLE
CONSERVATION HANDBOOK

Water Vole Conservation Handbook. © English Nature, Environment Agency, Wildlife Conservation Research Unit. 1998.

Opportunities for Nature

Scotland supports nearly 90,000 different species, thousands of which live in or near our rivers and urban areas and interact with each other to form complex ecological communities. These are part of the rich biodiversity - the variety of life - which includes all the different types of living organisms, their genetic diversity and the communities they form. Rivers and burns are therefore much more than channels taking water from source to sea - for Scotland's wildlife they have a great many uses:

- places to live and reproduce
- sources of food and water
- corridors for movement

It is important to realise that the land adjacent to a burn may be just as important in habitat terms as the water itself.

A complex, interacting system

No one habitat is independent. The interactions between organisms in different habitats make up the complex ecological communities, as illustrated above. If one component of the community is disturbed or removed, for example by destroying a single habitat, many organisms may be affected, either directly or indirectly. This is the complexity of a rich and natural ecosystem, which in an urban area, can be brought to an abrupt end.

In built-up areas, damage to habitats and consequently biodiversity is very common. For example, oversimplification of the river channel is a particular problem which affects biodiversity - straight, steep sided concrete channels offer little in-stream habitat for animals or plants. In addition, bankside habitat is often completely absent or severely restricted, and bridges, weirs, and culverts may block the movement of species both in and beside the water.

The protection and appropriate management of existing stretches of semi-natural river and burn corridors is therefore a priority in built-up areas. Restoration of downgraded stretches is also a realistic proposal in some situations. The recreation of 'natural' river corridors in all towns and villages would be impossible, but techniques to maximise biodiversity potential are feasible in many watercourses, and with long-term planning, restoration is a very real possibility.

Control the situation & make the most of the opportunity

Prevent and intercept pollution

- introduce Sustainable Urban Drainage techniques to prevent pollution from surface water drains draining directly into watercourses
- people need to realise the damage caused by disposing of waste in watercourses, and the penalties they face if caught.

Ensure the watercourse is as natural as practicable

- ensure that the flow characteristics of the watercourse are as natural as possible. Where dealing with an urban watercourse which is prone to flash flooding, tackle the problem by introducing Sustainable Urban Drainage techniques to reduce the flow at source.
- ensure there are decent wildlife habitats both in and next to the

watercourse, such as pools, gravel beds, riffles, river margins, and vegetation, both in and outside the water.

- provide suitable habitats, if habitats have been degraded, through seeking advice from ecologists.
- if modifying degraded systems, provide variation in stream and bank habitat structures, such as riffles, pools, gravel beds and vegetation.

Ensure wildlife can move along the watercourse and its banks

Otter. © SEPA

Apart from the provision of living space and food for organisms, river and burn corridors also provide vitally important routes for the movement of aquatic and terrestrial wildlife. For example, pollen from plants may be dispersed by the water, migratory fish such as Atlantic salmon and sea trout range over enormous distances during their lifecycles and require access to the upper reaches of watercourses to spawn. Otters travel long distances in search of food. If there is an obstacle in the urban section of the watercourse, the value of the upstream habitat can be threatened and even eliminated.

- a single watercourse can affect a large area upstream and downstream.
- the cost of restoring an urban watercourse will normally be more than recouped by an increase in the value of surrounding property and by a reduction in the long-term costs of maintenance.
- pollution in watercourses can also hazard human health, and can contaminate groundwater - which is worth tackling in its own right.
- make sure the watercourse provides a through route! Work to remove weirs, underground sections, concrete lined sections etc.
- retain areas for the sole use of wildlife. Because wildlife can easily be disturbed, it is important to provide areas where animals and plants can remain as undisturbed as possible.

See the end sections for more information on how to do it, regulations and much more.

Dipper. © Laurie Campbell, SNH

Pollution will reduce the biodiversity potential of a watercourse

- **Untreated and/or diluted sewage** - can enter the watercourse from combined sewage overflows and via wrong connections into surface water drainage systems. The combination of toxic effects, nutrient enrichment and reduced oxygen levels in the watercourse may severely impact water quality and kill wildlife.
- **Nitrates** - used in agriculture and arising from many other urban sources, can cause algal blooms and unsightly excessive higher plant growth within the channel.
- **Phosphates** - used in washing powders and as fertilisers in agriculture and forestry can also cause excess growth of bottom living algae and higher plants, leading to severely reduced oxygen levels.
- **Oils and Solvents** - are occasionally accidentally and sometimes deliberately disposed of down drains which discharge into watercourses. These may be toxic to aquatic life, and can also build up in time in sediments on the river bottom, thus also having a long term impact.
- **Heavy metals** - include lead and vanadium, some originate from road run-off from cars and lorries. Heavy metals can accumulate in sediment.
- **Other road debris** - includes dog faeces, tyre debris, grit, salt and effluent, from wheelie bin cleaners and people washing their cars and so on.
- **Heavy sediment loads** - normally caused by interference with a watercourse, changes in catchment land-use leading to excess erosion, or building works near a river. Sediments can smother and kill vegetation and invertebrates, as well as suffocate fish by blocking their gills and preventing them from taking in oxygen from the water.

Points to watch

- **Wildlife preservation** - the majority of watercourses have some wildlife - be careful and make every attempt not to damage what is already there
- **Value is not always obvious** - healthy rivers are not always pretty! Clearing dead vegetation can also remove valuable habitat niches along the riverbanks.

The Richness of Rivers

A Scottish river ecosystem is the product of thousands of years of evolution and interaction of water, rock and life. The erosion and deposition of sediments is continually creating and recreating over a range of timescales an enormous variety of aquatic, marginal, riparian and floodplain habitats with a rich biota that has evolved to live in, and help shape, these unique conditions over thousands of years. The functioning of both the biological and the geomorphological systems together describe the river ecosystem. It is important to note that the aquatic and "terrestrial" components in an intact river ecosystem are interdependent- sediments deposited on the floodplains build the soils and their fertility; in meandering areas the changing channel of the river creates natural ponds, swamp, fen and carr habitats.

(1) Nutrients washing off the land, insects and vegetation help provide energy for aquatic animals and plants. (2) Many species such as mayflies and stoneflies have an aquatic and an airborne stage, and inhabit the dry areas around the channel during their lifecycle. Other species, such as bats (3) and sandmartins, reap the benefits of the insects emerging from their aquatic life-cycle stages. Sandmartins and the fish feeding kingfishers (4) of southern Scotland, further exploit the natural eroding cliffs created by rivers to build their nests (5). These habitats and others, such as lush grassy banks, bank-side tree roots, over- hanging boughs (6), tall emergent grasses (7), and cobble and rocky shores provide nests and shelter areas for a myriad of other species - including dippers (8), water voles (9) and otters (10) which feed on the rich food stores of the river. Care must therefore be taken not to adversely impact the important terrestrial habitats adjacent to a river when carrying out river works.

Opportunities for People

The water environment can play a positive role in our lives, in terms of education, relaxation, recreation and so on. © *MPB*

Salmon fishing. © *Lorne Gill, SNH*

A restored river which combines cycle and footpaths. Run footpaths along one side of the river so people can enjoy its beauty, while wildlife can enjoy seclusion. © *RRC*

Benefits for people

Our towns and cities need to offer the highest quality of life and the highest quality environments that we can manage. Water can play a decisive part in bringing that about.

Something to look at and enjoy

Water regularly features high in the list of things people like to look at. Where people have set out to make a beautiful environment, such as city parks, or even landscape paintings, water is a common and delightful feature. Commercial companies realise the importance of addressing high-order human needs in marketing their products. The same needs to apply to our built up areas.

- People look at the reflections in the water, of the sky, of buildings or trees, and the ever changing surface of the water;
- people absorb the tranquillity and a watercourse may be the only piece of natural beauty in a central urban area;
- people observe wildlife - below the surface, on the surface, on the banks and in the air;
- people fish - one of society's most popular forms of recreation;
- children paddle, fish, throw stones, make boats, play games, build dams, swing out over the water on ropes;
- on some rivers people can canoe, row, sail or motor.

A route for people

Watercourses can form the basis of a network of footpaths and cycleways:

- **Direct routes** - the most popular routes are those which take pedestrians in the direction they want to go. Often a watercourse will cut through an urban area, and providing access along it, such as a footpath or a cycleway, can provide an invaluable route into central areas.
- **Attractive, healthier routes** - the quiet of a burn-side walk compares with the noise and pollution of a walk next to a road.
- **Safe routes** - no risk from traffic. Consider other security issues, including surveillance and lighting where appropriate.

Provide public access paths, suitable for disabled users. *River Skerne, Darlingon* © *RRC*

Something to study

Wildlife around watercourses is particularly rich, and relatively easy to observe. Watercourses offer an opportunity for people of all ages to learn and understand more about the environment. Consider:

- creating dipping platforms on suitable areas of watercourse, perhaps in association with a local school;
- providing information boards which explain the wildlife that can be found in the immediate vicinity, the type of habitat, and the local history, eg location of old mills;
- highlighting the Local Biodiversity Action Plan, to show local people what it all about.

Control the situation & make the most of the opportunity

Make the watercourse safe and people friendly

- keep the risks in perspective - we don't fence off our roads and streets, why then should we fence off burns and rivers;
- ensure children learn to swim and understand both the delights and dangers;
- where appropriate grade back steep banks, consider installing two-stage channels with reed ledges, etc;
- provide ladders, grab rails etc on channelled sections;
- ensure security of culvert grills is regularly checked;
- avoid hidden and neglected watercourses - those watercourses which are cared for and overseen are safer.

Make the watercourse attractive

- get rid of the hard utilitarian features, and make the watercourse look as natural and attractive as possible;
- leave alone any remaining relatively untouched sections of river;
- make sure people can see the water. Some watercourses lie well below the level of the land, often due to human intervention. Check the relative levels of the watercourse and the surrounding land or footpaths - people should ideally be no more than about two metres above the level of the watercourse. After taking suitable ecological advice, consider grading back slopes if the watercourse is deeply set into the floodplain - or consider raising the bed of the watercourse. Flood levels should be considered when changing the level of footpaths or land. In some cases it is better to have a gentle bank and yearly flooding, than a harsh constricted watercourse with steep banks, and fast flowing water.

Local Biodiversity Action Plans generally led by local authority

Biodiversity in Scotland - The Way Forward 1997

UK Biodiversity Action Plan 1994

Convention on Biological Diversity Earth Summit - Rio 1992

Biodiversity Framework Think Globally - Act Locally

Little girl paddling. © RPH

Points to watch

- **Personal security** - people have to be comfortable about using a route. How they feel is a combination of many different factors - women tend to be concerned about individuals, men tend to be more concerned about groups of youths; neglect such as allowing litter to collect, not repairing vandalism, can all serve to increase people's unease. Paths need to be designed, managed and maintained with personal security in mind.
- **Security of property** - creating a new footpath or cycle way can create fears over the possibility of new routes for burglars or vandals into surrounding property. This can be a significant source of objection to a new scheme. Options include introducing fencing, or better still, using natural planting and materials to create a barrier. The actual security risk may be less than people perceive. Increasing pedestrian movements is one way of reducing burglary and vandalism through improved surveillance.
- **Retaining areas for wildlife** - people and domestic pets can disturb animal life. If public access is provided, consider reserving areas exclusively for wildlife. There may be stretches along watercourses in the urban area where access for people should ideally not be encouraged, due to the presence of rare animals and plant species.

The River Ness running through Inverness. Many towns and cities have grown on the banks of rivers. The rivers can continue to play a unique part in the character of these urban centres. © *Graham Burns, SCP*

Opportunities for the Built Environment

Water and buildings combine to make some of the finest vistas in the world, but the setting does not have to be grand. A small burn can add charm and interest to what would otherwise be an undistinguished development. Much emphasis is now being placed on the importance of urban design, of making places which really work, where the buildings complement each other, where the spaces in between the buildings are both functional and attractive. Similarly watercourses and the areas surrounding buildings need to be designed to complement each other. Urban design matters, and watercourses matter in terms of urban design.

However, it is often the case that building goes on, not merely ignoring the benefits of water, but ignoring the threats it can pose. The development of a town should, at the very minimum, show respect for the power of its watercourses; and ideally should embrace them.

Build to embrace watercourses

Ideally urban areas should be built to reflect the local topography, and especially the watercourses that run through it. Watercourses can be made a feature of urban developments, rather than treated as a problem. Benefits include:
- a more marketable, higher value development;
- greater attractiveness - on a global scale there are a number of cities which pride themselves on the mix of architecture and water.

Aerial view of Linlithgow. © *Lorne Gill, SNH*

In a new development where there is a watercourse which is in natural condition, it should be left in that state to maintain its value for wildlife and as a landscape feature. In existing developments there are opportunities for restoring watercourses as part of redevelopment schemes. Hard and soft landscaping can, with careful thought, provide a fine setting for buildings and a much improved natural habitat.

Control the situation and make the most of the opportunity

Use urban watercourses to enhance the built environment

- ensure new developments focus on watercourses, and use them as assets - as a natural one which provides conservation value, and as a human one which gives delight to the surrounding buildings;
- consider reintroducing watercourses as a focus in existing developments;
- use the space occupied by watercourses to create vistas - large expanses of water can provide a magnificent setting for buildings and bridges.

Incorporation of a water feature at Aviemore. © *RPH (when planning such features be careful not to impede the passage of fish)*

Do not ignore watercourse frontages

- treat the waterfrontage as the highest value land in the urban area;
- avoid using urban rivers as a main road corridor - noise and pollution will greatly reduce the value to the community - plant, animal and human!

- do not block off banks with high walls or six foot fences - keep them gently sloping, open and accessible.

Use watercourses to create interest in the urban fabric

- small scale features - eg a burn running down one side of the road for a short length, a glimpse of a burn through a gap in a wall;
- create public spaces next to a watercourse, allowing wildlife their own space in the process;
- landscaping can be hard or soft, intimate or open;
- spaces can be bordered by:
  houses or flats;
  shops, pubs and restaurants;
  commercial development.

Introduce Sustainable Urban Drainage Systems in all new developments and progressively introduce them in existing developments

See chapter four, on working with water

Housing estate with adjacent watercourse used to create an atractive pedestrian route to other parts of town. © RPH

Appropriate urban landuse - the park in Cupar, Fife, floods with some frequency. Controlled flooding in such areas is likely to reduce flooding to residentual and industrial premises downstream. © A R Black

Points to watch

• Where to develop

National Planning Policy Guidance 7 gives clear guidance:
"Development of an area which is exposed to frequent or extensive flooding is likely to be unsustainable and should be avoided... (NPPG7)
Where development is essential the threat of flooding should be managed in an environmentally sensitive way. The role of soft engineering measures such as natural flood meadows and washlands in attenuating flooding should be recognised, and additional flood protection measures should only be adopted after consideration of all available techniques which can provide the appropriate level of protection...."

Check that the local development plan does not zone development within a floodplain.

• What about brownfield sites on the floodplain?

If it is a single development within the floodplain, and is either causing significant problems downstream, or is costing a great deal in flood defence works, it may be more cost effective to abandon the site.
If it is a brownfield site within a heavily developed floodplain, make sure the development proposals make use of the watercourse for both nature and human benefit. Consider the possibility for uses for the site, and designs for buildings, which avoid the need for, flood protection measures.

• Avoid damage to natural watercourses

Sometimes people think that unless the watercourse is "put into a pipe" there will be a risk of flooding to the development.
There have been numerous incidents of serious local flooding being caused by culverts, which have become blocked during a storm. Branches and debris and litter are carried downstream, collect on the grills at the entrance to the culvert and block it. One major flood was caused by a discarded television set and a door jamming about 40 metres down a pipe.
Nature's way is the best and safest way. Natural, sustainable drainage techniques are normally cheaper to install and maintain. The cost of employing professionals to produce an ecologically sensitive landscape design and sustainable drainage system for a new development can be easily recouped by increased property values and in the distinctiveness of the development.

Incorporation of Sustainable Urban Drainage techniques in a housing development at Kirknewton, West Lothian. © G McKissock

Watercourses can also be enhanced to benefit people as below. Ideally, both should be accomplished. © RPH

3 Some Ideas on Applying the Techniques

This section provides some ideas on what to do with various types of watercourse under different circumstances. In all instances it is important to:

- consider the whole catchment - where there are likely to be effects;
- avoid damaging existing habitats;
- make sure the proposals work, as well as look good;
- balance human need with nature;
- produce an original, thought-through scheme rather than copy other schemes or practices.

All new developments - an opportunity to use Sustainable Urban Drainage Systems (SUDS)

Thousands of pounds can be saved in new developments by using SUDS. By reducing run-off, the need for expensive new piped drainage systems can be reduced or even avoided. The techniques reduce pollution of watercourses and downstream flooding. Some SUDS incorporating ponds and swales can increase the attractiveness of a development. Equipping new houses with water storage butts from the outset may also reduce run-off.

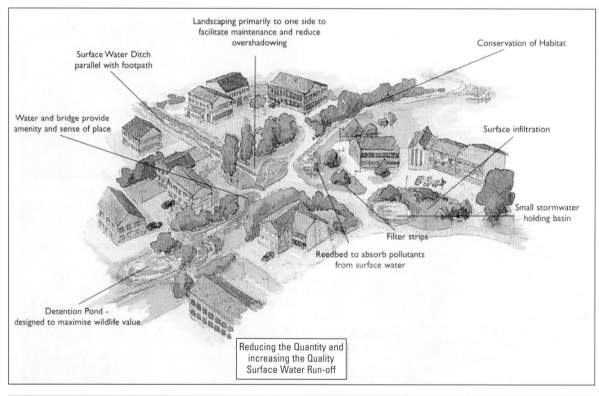

Landscaping primarily to one side to facilitate maintenance and reduce overshadowing

Conservation of Habitat

Surface Water Ditch parallel with footpath

Surface infiltration

Water and bridge provide amenity and sense of place

Small stormwater holding basin

Filter strips

Reedbed to absorb pollutants from surface water

Detention Pond - designed to maximise wildlife value

Reducing the Quantity and increasing the Quality Surface Water Run-off

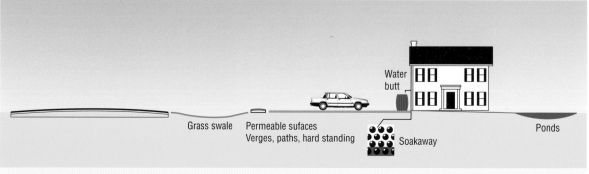

Water butt

Grass swale   Permeable sufaces
Verges, paths, hard standing

Soakaway

Ponds

Some examples of sustainable urban drainage features that could be applied to an everyday house.

New greenfield or brownfield housing development - with small burn

In the past - developers would have buried the burn in an underground culvert or pipe and then overlayed a standard road layout over the site, working in as many houses as possible, and making sure the largest possible vehicles could be accommodated easily.

The result has been residential estates that have very little character and little variation.

Alternative - adjust the development so that the burn becomes its focus, rather than the road network.

Worked example

Use the latest guidance on the layout of residential roads - eg Places Streets and Movement DETR 1998 (Supplement to Design Bulletin 32 Layout of residential roads and footpaths) - to produce a housing layout that maximises the attractiveness of the public spaces and the natural features of the site, including the burn, then work in the road layout ensuring minimum recommended tracking dimensions are obtained.

Consider:
- houses with their fronts to the burn, and their backs to the access roads, the area either side of the burn providing open space and a safe pedestrian route;
- making a pond as central feature for the development, to provide retention and detention of flood waters and to improve the quality of run-off from the development, before it flows into the watercourse;

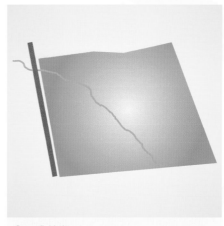

Greenfield site

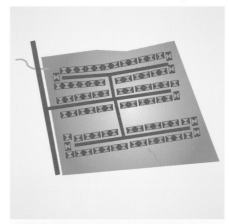

Standard approach based on cul-de-sac and buried watercourse.

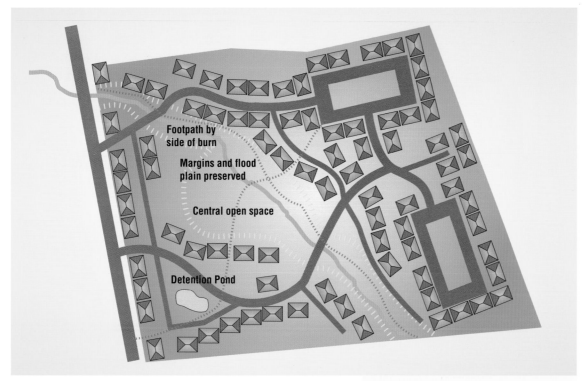

Footpath by side of burn

Margins and flood plain preserved

Central open space

Detention Pond

An alternative approach with the burn as the focus

- using sustainable drainage systems rather than pipes and channels to drain the roads and areas of hard standing - consider pervious surfaces and swales, wetlands and ponds;
- creating footpaths along the watercourse to connect with other areas, considering long term possibilities - even though a through access may not be possible at present, it might in 20 years time - produce a design that keeps the options open.

Watercourse running along a street

In a number of towns and villages a burn or river runs under, or next to, the street. Often the watercourse is placed in an underground culvert, but in a few places the watercourse still runs on the surface providing an attractive feature and maintaining value to wildlife.

Town centres

In town centres, see if it is possible to break out the watercourse so that if forms a focal point of the town. With changes in shopping patterns, including tele-shopping and electronic commerce, the leisure element of shopping will become increasingly important. What better way to improve the quality of people's experience in town centres than to add water?

Where a watercourse runs along a main street, a combination of hard and soft landscaping could create something that is appropriate to the town centre, yet still provide value to nature and avoids creating a barrier to fish. Provide access for disabled people to the water's edge.

Work in an urban centre can be costly and affordable by only the most determined communities. However, like those who protect their assets in the first place, they will be rewarded in the future.

Other areas

Surface watercourses should be retained wherever possible and managed to provide the maximum practicable benefit for the people who live in the town, and for the wildlife that lives or moves in the water.

Small burns running alongside roads are sometimes culverted because people believe they collect litter. The result is that a useful habitat is lost by a lack of human care for the built environment. Litter, once discarded, has to go somewhere. If there is a problem with litter, the cure is to stop the litter, not to remove the places where it collects. Make sure the relevant legislation is being enforced.

Keep the watercourses in the open.
Even though the habitat value of this watercourse is limited, at least it provides a visual amenity to the local inhabitants. There is much scope to increase the value to nature. © SEPA

Watercourse crossing the street

Creating new routes for people

Where a burn or river runs across a street, there may be an opportunity to provide new routes for pedestrians and cyclists.

In a town centre, a riverside walk could be an excellent way of linking a town centre car park to the main shopping centre.

In a residential area, the river or burn corridor might be ideal for providing a new pedestrian or cycle route.

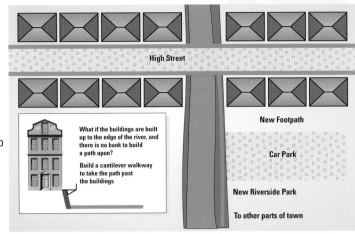

High Street

What if the buildings are built up to the edge of the river, and there is no bank to build a path upon?

Build a cantilever walkway to take the path past the buildings

New Footpath

Car Park

New Riverside Park

To other parts of town

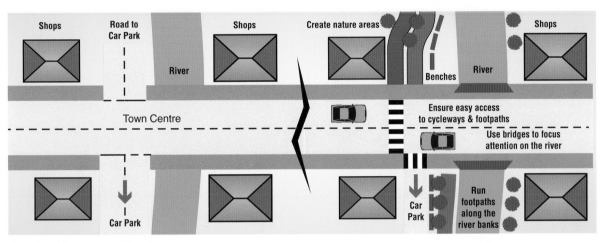

Shops | Road to Car Park | Shops | Create nature areas | Shops

River | Benches | River

Town Centre

Ensure easy access to cycleways & footpaths

Use bridges to focus attention on the river

Car Park

Car Park | Run footpaths along the river banks

Creating Vistas in residential areas

An everyday residential street can be transformed by retaining views of a burn.

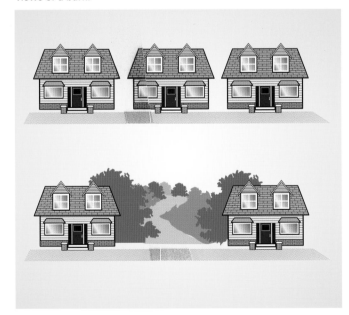

Creating Vistas in the centre of town

A roadside waterfall turned into a feature by the addition of a stone arch. The result - centuries of pleasure for people passing by. © RPH

Town centre separated from river by a road

Many UK towns have their waterfronts marred by transport infrastructure. This may have been expedient at one time, but if the town needs to expand or to improve its attractiveness or distinctiveness, the presence of a major riverside road can be a fatal obstacle.

Investigate options for significantly reducing the traffic along the road, aiming to allow some through traffic but also making it more pleasant for people: safe, reasonably quiet and pollution free.

Investigate options for locating the road away from the river. It is likely to be a long term process - possibly taking decades. It is important not to use a river corridor as a major transport route in the first place.

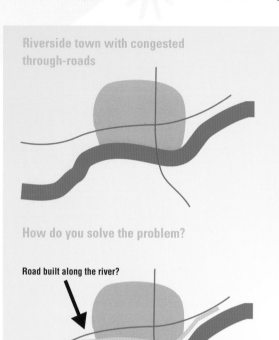

Riverside town with congested through-roads

How do you solve the problem?

Road built along the river?

Alternatives avoiding the river

It is better to look for an option that solves today's problems while creating opportunities for the future as well - even though it might cost more in the short term.

Many towns have been built by rivers; some taking advantage of a strategic crossing, others making use of the defensive value of the river, or its potential as a means of transporting goods.

Growth in traffic can mean that environmental conditions within the town become unpleasant, and congestion becomes a significant problem.

The traditional solution would be to build a road along the river corridor, through the river flood plain and through what is likely to be industrial riverside development, wharves etc. In the past this type of option will have been chosen because it is:
• cheapest
• most direct
• likely to raise objections from fewer people.

But - building a road between the town and the river cuts off the town from what may be one of its most important assets and brings to a close any potential the river might have played in the future development of the town.

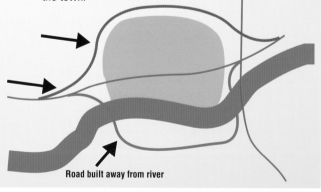

Road built away from river

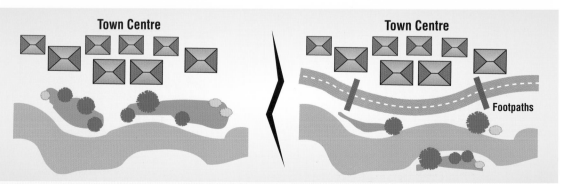

Consider potential for traffic reduction. If a road is necessary, find a route around the river keeping away from the river margins.

If there is no alternative to building a road along the river frontage, pay close attention to preserving as much of its habitat and attractiveness as possible.

Edge of town centre

Watercourse running through a mix of developments on the edge of the town centre

In these less high profile areas there are likely to be fewer resources available to get things done.

Aim to create a cycle and pedestrian route along the watercourse. Where desirable, re-profile the banks to remove steep drops or form a two-stage channel; this can also provide pedestrians and cyclists with a better view of the watercourse. Introduce riffles and, where space permits, meanders. As always, seek sound ecological advice before commencing and establish what habitat and species are present which may need protection.

River surrounded by low value development which makes no use of its presence

(eg watercourse edged in by car parks, warehouses, possibly derelict areas - brownfield sites etc).
Encourage redevelopment which allows the watercourse to be made of value to both wildlife and the community. Establish a long term policy in the local development plan for the rehabilitation of the watercourse. Consider re-designating the land for alternative land uses, eg housing, shops, leisure. Include the provision of full pedestrian and cycling access. Consider whether it would be better to cease the use of the site altogether and return it to nature especially if it is within the floodplain.

An industrial estate

Small river at the back of industrial estate, in concrete channel

Option
Use the watercourse as the basis for a new pedestrian and cycle route into the industrial estate from adjoining residential areas, aiming to reduce traffic. Encourage land owners to make more positive use of watercourse frontage.

Residential areas

Fenced-off surface level watercourse with maintenance access strip running through residential area

(typical 1930's suburban housing estate).
Option
Subject to consultation, create a public footpath along the maintenance strip. Where the watercourse has been artificially deepened, consider the possibility of lowering the maintenance strip to reduce the height of the bank.

Watercourse running at the back of people's gardens - no public access

Encourage residents to respect the watercourse, and to incorporate positively into their gardens. Suggest techniques which would allow greater conservation value. Warn them of the consequences of fly-tipping into the burn.

Water can provide a delightful setting for housing, offices or light industry - but building on flood plains should be avoided, owing to the risk of flooding. It is also against planning guidance.

A constrained burn at Dornoch. Although development right up to the river margins has reduced the wildlife value and increased flood risk, the burn is clearly valued by the community. © SEPA

Housing by Leithen Water, with the houses facing onto the water, gives amenity value yet should also seek to leave river margins largely undisturbed. © SEPA

Inhospitable, dull watercourse in a park

Parks are ideal places to support a natural watercourse. Normally, there is plenty of space for a different range of habitats, and to let the watercourse settle into its own course. However, many parks and recreation grounds have over maintained watercourses - straightened, reprofiled using excavators, or even constrained by brick or concrete lined channels. The surrounding trees and vegetation can appear stark, not only to people, but also to wildlife.

Plant trees to provide shading to reduce weed growth and provide visual interest. Trees will also help reduce wind-speed in the park, which will make it more comfortable to use for a greater portion of the year.

Natural processes

Discontinue excavator works and allow watercourse to stabilise on its own (1).
The watercourse will slowly return to a natural profile if natural erosion and deposition of material can take place (2-3); bankside vegetation will help stabilise banks. A close watch should be kept on the watercourse to see that, should the sides of the bank slump, there is no unacceptable increase in the risk of flood damage to property, or adverse environmental impact. The diagrams below show a three-stage process by which the stream may naturally stabilise without the need for intervention.

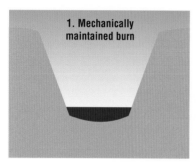
1. Mechanically maintained burn

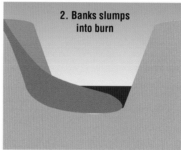
2. Banks slumps into burn

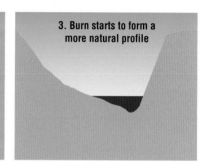
3. Burn starts to form a more natural profile

Intervention

If the burn has been heavily degraded and constrained by concrete, it will be necessary to intervene, and start the natural recovery process.
Re-profile banks and vary the channel, to create a more natural form. Gently shelving edges can help people exit from the water should they fall in. Consider the possibility of creating a two-stage channel. This increases flood storage and conveyance. Consider creating off-line ponds.

Restoring a channelled burn

Urban stream in park, with brick-lined bank.
© SEPA

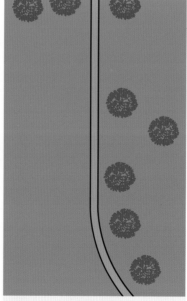
Urban stream in park, with brick-lined bank (plan view)
- lost opportunity for both people and nature
- provided at considerable cost
- maintenance - on-going

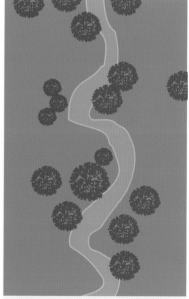
Urban stream in park, brick-lined bank removed - natural profile, with meanders reinstated
- attractive to both people and wildlife
- cost - negligible
- maintained by natural processes
- allows controlled flooding within park area helping to reduce flooding downstream

Some Ideas on Applying the Techniques

Restoring a channelled burn

Where space is too restricted to allow the watercourse room to wander and the burns are channelled, natural forms of bank protection using willow spilling etc, can sometimes be utilised as a more habitat friendly option than steel, concrete or wooden board. In-stream habitat structures can also be used to increase biological diversity - these give the watercourse some of the characteristics of a natural burn. Deflectors, gravel banks, or riffles, fixed or anchored cover structures, such as interwoven willow branches, gabions, or granite rubble or even randomly placed rocks in the channel bed can produce changes in water velocity as well as bed character. Selecting which are most appropriate usually requires some input from specialists such as hydrogeomorphologists.

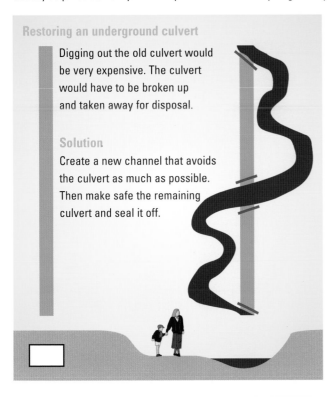

Restoring an underground culvert

Digging out the old culvert would be very expensive. The culvert would have to be broken up and taken away for disposal.

Solution
Create a new channel that avoids the culvert as much as possible. Then make safe the remaining culvert and seal it off.

Banks can be set aside to provide habitats for rare animals such as water voles eg Glasgow City Council have made considerable efforts to safeguard the habitat of these rare species during flood defence works. Have regard to species protection from disturbance under Wildlife and Countryside Act 1981 - refer to SNH for further guidance.

A rare water vole protected rather than destroyed by human activities. © R. Strachan, The Environment Agency

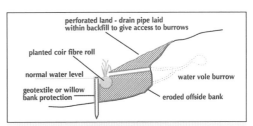

Much can be achieved by carrying out wildlife surveys before work commences in order that suitable habitat protection measures can be included. (Preservation of water vole burrows. Watervole Conservation Handbook © English Nature, Environment Agency and the Wildlife Conservation Research Unit, 1998)

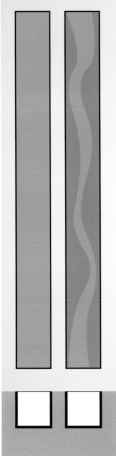

Increasing the habitat value of a channelled watercourse

Concrete lined channelled watercourses often provide insufficient depth of water in normal weather to support a wide range of wildlife. In storm conditions most of the life in the channel is washed out by the force of the water. Without reeds, shallows, backwaters, etc, there is no refuge for wildlife. A channelled watercourse can be improved by putting artificial riffles into the channel to restrict the flow and create a varying depth of water. Professional help should be obtained to avoid the risk of reducing the capacity of the watercourse and increasing upstream flooding, or alternatively failing to install sufficiently robust structures, which are then washed out and cause blockages downstream.

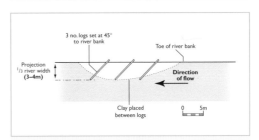

Enhancing straightened river channels. Type A deflector (Plan View). Manual of River Restoration Techniques © RRC

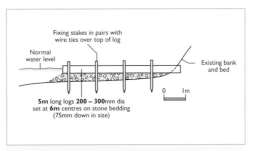

Type A deflector. Section through log. Manual of River Restoration Techniques © RRC

4. Working with Water

In Scotland, urban watercourses range from large powerful rivers to small burns which rise within urban areas. Many offer great potential for improvement, but the key to their improvement is an understanding of natural catchment processes and the use of the full range of modern techniques for working with water.

All of the different aspects interrelate. An action in one area will result in a reaction elsewhere.

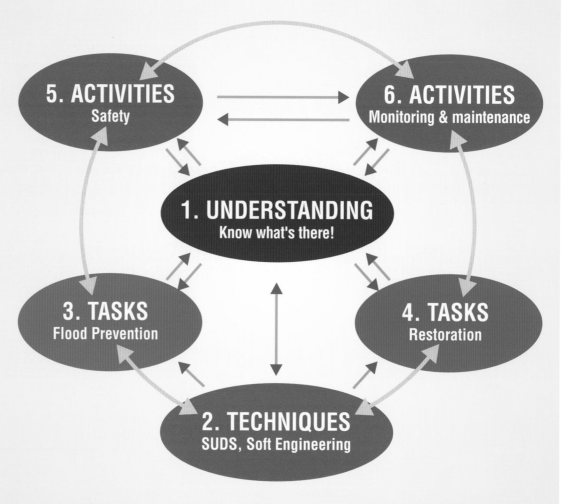

Working with water requires a basic understanding of the principles involved.

The numbers in the diagram relate to the steps described in this chapter. Whichever step you start at, the natural cycle will eventually lead you through them all.

Step 1 - Understanding

Knowledge of burns, rivers and catchments

Few people, when they look at a burn or a river, perceive the complexity and power of the water. Over thousands of years, a complex relationship develops between the flow of water, the form of the landscape, the animals and plants, and the water chemistry. The study of these relationships is the subject of specialist scientific disciplines, including:

- fluvial geomorphology
- ecology
- hydrology
- biochemistry

Together, these sciences are providing us with a far better understanding of rivers, and the resulting effects of human intervention.

The following descriptions are examples which show the sort of problems that could arise before we developed an understanding:

During the Victorian period in Scotland, to improve the drainage of a piece of land a meandering river was often replaced by a cut which provided a shorter path for the water, but at a much steeper gradient. No sooner had the new cut been opened than the rapid flow of water would severely erode the banks and deposit new sediments in the lower sections, causing new problems downstream.

In the 1930s, towns which were subject to flooding were often protected by the deepening and widening of the river. However, the deepened section would often rapidly fill with gravel carried down by the river from upstream. The maintenance of the section would in some instances involve the removal each year of several thousand tonnes of gravel.

It must be remembered that rivers are ruled by the forces of nature. They adjust their channel dimensions, gradients and meanders in relation to flow and sediments. Irrespective of what man does, nature will try to restore this natural equilibrium. The trick is to use expertise to do what nature would do in the first place. There are three tasks:

- make the drainage system more natural;
- ensure the watercourses are as natural as possible;
- avoid confronting nature by building on land prone to flooding.

Step 2 - Techniques

Source control techniques can be used to control and reduce run-off from new urban development. These techniques can also be used to remove pollutants from the water.

The techniques reduce flooding by slowing the rate at which the rain discharges into watercourses. By slowing the flow, some of the suspended solids in the water settle out and bacteria, microbes and larger plants have time to reduce the nutrient levels in the water, and tackle some of the other pollutants - so that when the water finally reaches a watercourse the level of contamination is much reduced. Some of the techniques also help to replenish ground water; this also helps to sustain summer flows in watercourses.

Applying the science

Rivers are complicated systems that we need to incorporate and plan for at a catchment scale. When we do make a substantial intervention we need to be using the best information from an integrated science.

Fluvial geomorphology
the study of the evolution of landforms shaped by rivers and the processes involved has given us a far better understanding of the role of erosion and the deposition of gravels and other sediments.

Biochemistry
how the chemistry of the water can be affected by changes in the drainage pattern, in the use of fertilisers, pollution from development (including phosphates from washing machines and people washing their cars and wheelie bins which, via road drains, discharge directly into rivers), plus more subtle biochemical changes that can be caused by interfering with the bed of the watercourse or its banks.

Ecology
has brought an understanding of the interdependence of organisms and habitats, and how a single watercourse can affect wildlife far beyond its immediate banks.

Hydraulic modelling
can be used to predict the effect of changes in the watercourse, such as deepening a channel, straightening a watercourse or introducing flood embankments. Because of the complexity of watercourses and catchments, it is important that no major changes are made to watercourses, floodplains or flood protection embankments without using these tools to consider both the local impact and the impact on the whole catchment.

By using urban drainage systems upstream, pictures like this could be come a thing of the past. © RPH

Natural engineering techniques

A definition

A new approach which works with nature
- uses the natural process that shapes the river environment
- reduces maintenance costs
- reduces damage to the environment

It is an inter-disciplinary approach between ecologists, fluvial geomorphologists, hydrologists and engineers.

It seeks sustainable solutions by reducing maintenance and minimising negative off-site effects.

It incorporates multiple objectives (protection and enhancement of biodiversity and public amenity) rather than having the single issue focus of traditional river management.

It has a low risk of failure.

Because it is multi-objective, it draws on the community to help define what they want in the context of advice from the specialists on what is possible.

The choice of the most appropriate techniques depends on the availability of land, the type of soil, the sensitivity of watercourses. Guidance is given in the CIRIA Sustainable urban drainage systems design manual C521.

Tackle water at source - where the rain hits the ground

These techniques are effective at removing much of the pollution from road run-off.

Limit directly drained surfaces

Growth in car ownership is resulting in an increase in the proportion of land in urban areas that is paved. Run-off can be reduced by ensuring these paved areas drain onto porous surfaces including grass swales etc. Gravel can also be used for hard standing as an alternative to concrete, tarmac or paving block surfacing.

Rainfall from building roofs can be intercepted by waterbutts, and soakaways. Every little helps in reducing peak flows in local burns, and the benefits transfer downstream, by reducing flash flooding.

Porous pavements

Porous paving materials can be used for carparks and footways, which allow water to percolate through into the ground rather than flowing straight into a drain. They help avoid the need for drains and the public liability problems associated with them.

Porous paving can significantly reduce surface water run-off.
© SEPA Natures Way

Infiltration pits or trenches, filter drains, storage in pervious blankets

Water from car parks, roads and roofs can be channelled into an infiltration layer. These help slow the flow and remove pollution.

Swales

Broad, shallow grass channels can be used instead of drains to convey water to a watercourse or treatment system - they slow the flow of water and provide some storage, allowing pollutants and silt to settle. Oil is intercepted by the grass where bacteria can then break it down. Swales are cheap to maintain by periodic mowing, but the grass needs to be removed to prevent choking.

Swales look good, are good for the environment, and are cheap to maintain. © SEPA Nature's Way

Infiltration trench

A device where water is stored temporarily to allow it to drain into the soil, or be channelled towards a network of detention or retention features as detailed below, improving water quality and adding to the attractiveness and habitat value.

Detention ponds

These are used to temporarily store surface water run-off to reduce flood flows in a watercourse and allow settling of silt - they can be designed to incorporate standing water to create wildlife habitats. Access for maintenance must be planned at the start of the project.

Retention ponds

These are ponds with permanent water, and wetland and aquatic vegetation. They can hold run-off for several days to allow a large proportion of the sediment to settle out, and enable some biological treatment of any pollution prior to release into a watercourse. Again, maintenance access must be planned.

Wetlands and reedbeds

Here surface water run-off is discharged into pond features which have a greater proportion of emergent vegetation such as reeds and rushes that help trap silt and sediment and filter pollutants from the water. Further guidance on the design of such systems is included in the reference section.

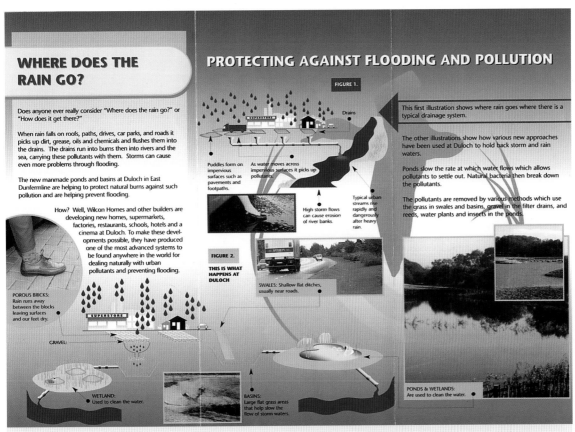

The role of education is very important in improving development practices. Information leaflet on Sustainable Urban Drainage Systems, Dulloch Park, Fife. *(extract from the leaflet published courtesy of Wilcon Homes)*

Step 3 - Tasks

Restoration

River restoration is very positive, but it should be undertaken with good advice. And it is not just major rivers that need restoration. Smaller burns often have the greatest potential for repair, and can make a great difference to the communities through which they flow. What is done should relate to the condition of the watercourse. It is normally best to let nature take its course. But urban watercourses can be so badly damaged that human works are needed.

Typical urban stream with concrete reinforced banks. © SEPA

Softer bank protection utilising an approach willow spilling technique. © Manual of River Restoration Techniques, RRC

Questions to ask yourself

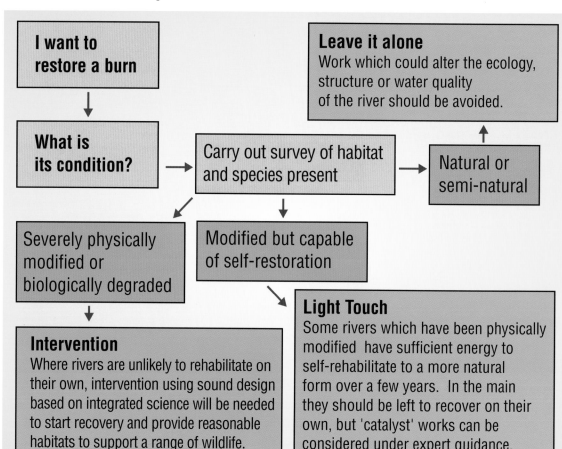

I want to restore a burn

↓

What is its condition? → Carry out survey of habitat and species present → Natural or semi-natural

↑

Leave it alone
Work which could alter the ecology, structure or water quality of the river should be avoided.

Severely physically modified or biologically degraded

Modified but capable of self-restoration

↓

Intervention
Where rivers are unlikely to rehabilate on their own, intervention using sound design based on integrated science will be needed to start recovery and provide reasonable habitats to support a range of wildlife.

Light Touch
Some rivers which have been physically modified have sufficient energy to self-rehabilitate to a more natural form over a few years. In the main they should be left to recover on their own, but 'catalyst' works can be considered under expert guidance.

Listed below are some of the measures that can be used to help restore a badly degraded watercourse.

Re-introduce riffles and pools

Riffles can be created by importing stone to concentrate flow and create deeper water upstream, fast flow at the constriction and self-scouring pools below.

Riffles aerate the water, which is important in summer when oxygen levels in the water can become depleted. Faster flowing, more turbulent sections provide a different type of habitat and can create the pleasant sound of running water which can help mask background traffic noise.

Pools can also be created by dredging to create habitats for fish, and other animals and plants, but unless they are dug in the right place, they will simply fill with sediment. Care must be taken not to reduce the carrying capacity of the watercourse and increase flooding risk.

Two stage channels - for summer and storm

Water levels in watercourses can vary dramatically through the year. Two-stage channels provide a first-stage self-scouring low flow channel which will support wildlife though the summer, and a second-stage high flow channel which increases channel capacity sufficiently to deal with storm flows. The second-stage section offers good habitat for marginal vegetation and wetland plants, such as reeds, iris, sedge etc.

Two-stage channel. © *Drawing Attention, RRC*

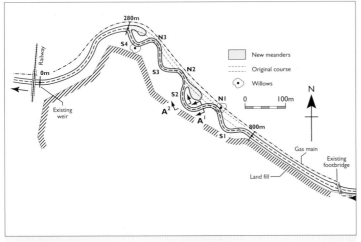

Re-introduce meanders. River Skerne restoration diagram. © *RRC*

Re-introduce meanders

The natural meanders of rivers flowing through flat plains slow down the flow and increase flood protection downstream. Re-introducing meanders brings the opportunity to create new riffles, point bars, and back-waters which are good habitats for a range of species. Selective planting of appropriate native species can be used to encourage wildlife and stabilise banks. Other effects may include increasing the tendency to flood upstream and along the reach; this is often intentional to reduce flooding in flood prone areas down-stream. New meanders may also change the transport of sediment along the watercourse. However:

- expert advice should be sought to avoid unwanted consequences;
- selective planting can be used to encourage wildlife and stabilise banks;
- backwaters can be created; they greatly enhance the visual interest of a restored watercourse, and are very effective at attracting amphibian and bird life.

Where there is little room to create a meander, selective planting of vegetation can create the illusion of a meander, and in-stream structures described above can create some of the habitats that a meander would have offered.

Removing culverts (daylighting) and concrete channels as part of urban renaissance and re-development schemes

The removal of a concrete culvert or channel (de-culverting or daylighting) can be expensive. If there is room, provide an alternative course for the burn or river. Meanders can be created by breaking through culverts at specific points. The rest of the culvert can be infilled and left alone.

Ponds

If space permits off-line ponds can be created. The best ones are made to be like the back waters of a traditional meandering watercourse. On-line ponds should always be avoided, as they increase the risk of downstream pollution during construction and maintenance. Pond margins should be constructed with a gentle slope and planted with reeds and rushes to discourage entry by children. Ponds do act as litter traps, and plans for litter collection should be made. Futher guidance on pond design can be found in the reference section.

Natural bank protection and stabilisation

Soft engineering techniques include the use of timber and natural materials, geotextiles etc. Willows can be very useful, and can be bundled or used as stakes. Cut sections of willows will sprout and this further stabilises the bank, giving a more natural appearance than concrete.

Landscaping can then be used to increase the recreational and amenity value of the river corridor.

Major schemes will require hydraulic modelling to predict the effects on the flow of the river and help ensure vegetation is not simply washed away.

Invisible outfalls

Traditionally designed outfalls can be among the most ugly structures along a watercourse. They give the public the impression that sewers are discharging into the water. Outfalls can be designed which discharge below the surface of the watercourse, while incorporating silt and oil traps. They still need to be carefully designed to prevent either siltation or erosion.

Further advice can be found in the River Restoration Centre *Manual of River Restoration Techniques*.

A healthy watercourse can support a wide range of wildlife. This is a large backwater formed by a sensitive river restoration scheme.
© *Manual of River Restoration Techniques, RRC*

Typical unsightly discharge to an urban stream.
© *RRC*

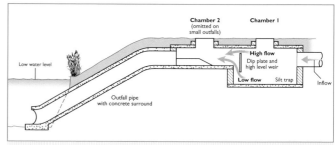

Diagram of sub-surface outfall - an invisible alternative. © *RRC*

New habitats in straightened channels

- introduce deflectors at normal water level to create mini-meanders, shoals, and areas of quiet water, and margins for plants;
- introduce riffles - a straight canalised watercourse can be very dull to look at and equally poor for river life;
- introduce ledges for aquatic plants, such as reeds and rushes.

New habitats in concrete-lined channels

- in-stream structures, such as pontoons, ledges or floating rafts, can be used but only as a last resort, to provide a platform for a wider range of wildlife in otherwise barren watercourses. They require careful design if they are not to be washed away, especially in flood conditions.

Restoring wildlife corridors

- by introducing a low flow channel and encouraging the deposition of natural material on the bed of the watercourse.

Step 4 - Tasks

Flood Prevention

The risk posed by upstream development

Urban development upstream will increase run-off and the risk of flooding downstream unless Sustainable Urban Drainage techniques are utilised (see the previous section on pages 26 and 27). It is important that these techniques are used extensively.

Control development in the flood plain

Flooding is a natural process and the flooding of property occurs because properties have been built in the flood plain. Planners and developers should be aware that a flood risk assessment provides a guide to the risk of flooding, not a guarantee against flooding. Planning applications should be assessed with flood risk in mind, and developers should be encouraged to consider using every topographical advantage of their site to minimise the effects of any floods.

Where development has taken place in a flood plain, be aware that flood defence measures can increase the risk of flooding downstream.

Physical measures

Flood banks

Flood defence banks should be built away from the natural channel (where space permits) to preserve the river margins and encourage habitat creation for such species as water voles and otters. By setting them back, they can be smaller, cheaper to construct and less visually intrusive, yet still contain the same flow.

Flood relief channels

Flood relief channels can be used to divert high flows away from a natural channel. Once freed of heavy storm flows, there are opportunities to re-profile and replant the natural channel. Examples can be obtained from the River Restoration Centre.

Culverting

Exceptionally, new culverts will be required, although developers will need to demonstrate that there is no alternative as well as incorporate fish passes. Ideally, follow the SEPA Policy on culverting and work to CIRIA Culvert Design Manual - CIRIA Report 168. If there is a need to cross a watercourse, a bridge may be less environmentally damaging and a more attractive option.

Flooding and 'soft' engineering

Government guidance on Planning and Flooding issued in National Planning Policy Guideline 7 in 1995 clearly recommends that 'the threat of flooding should be managed in an environmentally sensitive way. The role of soft engineering techniques such as natural flood meadows and washlands in attenuating flooding should be recognised and additional flood protection measures should only be adopted after full consideration of all available techniques which can provide the appropriate level of protection...'

Flooding can cause extensive damage to property and misery to the owners. © *G Burns, SCP*

What causes flooding?

Heavy rainfall over a large catchment - causing widespread flooding

Rapid melting of snow in the hills and mountains - major snow melts require a rapid rise in air temperature accompanied by heavy rain.

Summer thunderstorms which cause local flooding, especially in urban areas, where development has replaced absorbent fields and forests with rapidly draining surfaces such as roads and roofs.

Insufficient maintenance of man-made watercourses, culverts, gullies and other artificial drainage features.

Modifications to watercourses and floodplains which increase the speed at which water drains off the catchment, including canalisation, construction of flood embankments and changes in forestry and agricultural practices.

Urban development which reduces the amount of rainfall absorbed and increases the amount and rate at which it drains into watercourses.

What causes the flooding of property?
Inappropriate development within floodplains.

Road Safety vs Water Safety

The main difference between road safety and water safety is that on the roads or pavements one can be the victim of someone else's actions. Eight percent of pedestrian accidents occur while the pedestrian is on the pavement. Given the choice between encouraging people to spend time by the riverside, as opposed to the roadside, the riverside will be safer every time.

Natural watercourses vs man-made watercourses

Natural watercourses are inherently safer than man made drainage systems:

- they are less prone to flooding, especially flash flooding;
- there are no grills or pipes into which children can be attracted, and become trapped;
- the banks tend to be more gently sloping - making it easier for someone who has fallen in to clamber out.

Media coverage

Drownings in rivers and burns receive high profile press coverage because they are rare. On average, 10 people a day die on British roads, but the incidents go largely unreported. Nor are there calls for all roads to be fenced-off.

During summer days, such as this one below, water attracts people by the hordes. Safety in these kinds of situations is paramount.

When does a fun day out at the coast become a risk? We need to do all we can to ensure our children's safety by educating them about our environment.
© Doug Corrance, Still Moving Picture Company

Step 5 - Actions

Safety

The safety of urban watercourses can be a major public concern, particularly where people are hoping to restore a watercourse. There are risks involved with watercourses, and they should be logically assessed and where they do present a hazard, measures should be taken to reduce the hazard to a sensible level.

Human error - one of many causes of accidents

It is important to tackle safety as an issue that involves a number of solutions rather than going for a single solution approach. Most accidents involving water are the result of several different factors, and human error, misjudgement or misadventure normally figure highly. Some accidents occur because people are unaware of dangers or ignore the dangers, eg walking out over a frozen lake. Some occur where people overestimate their ability - such as swimming in cold water or because their attention is distracted. The number of accidents where water is the sole cause are small - an example might be a flash flood or an exceptionally severe flood.

Four routes to the safe enjoyment of watercourses

1. **Education** - sensible behaviour around watercourses needs to be part of the general education on the value of water, including the risks of ice, deep water and cold. The resulting effects of rubbish dumping, such as pollution and rats for example, should also be taught. (Education can also help people distinguish between disease carrying rats and threatened water vole communities).

2. **Changing the watercourse**
   - a bank with one in four slopes will normally allow people to clamber out;
   - use two-stage channels, to reduce steep gradients;
   - vegetation - reed shelves by the edge of the watercourse can act as a barrier to entry.

   Changes to the watercourse need to be carefully assessed as erosion and deposition further downstream can be an unintended consequence. In some instances, the danger will be man-made where the watercourse has been put into a concrete channel with vertical sides, making it hard to clamber out should an accident occur.

   Re-channelling should be approved before any action is taken, as it could cause unwanted scouring in areas of land, or even uncover landfill sites from years ago. Consult with the British Geological Society and 'Dial before you dig'.

3. **Safety aids** - such as grab rails, ladders, life-buoys can be included.

4. **Keeping people away from danger** - fencing or railing can be used to protect people from vertical drops, barrier planting can be also used. Low fencing can be used to halt toddlers.

Practical examples

Below are some examples of practical measures.

Falling down a steep bank and not being able to get out

Options:

- reprofile the bank so that it is no longer steep;
- lower the bank to remove the drop altogether;
- if there is no room for reprofiling, put a fence or hedge at the top of the bank and ensure vandal proof safety equipment is available;
- other plants which prevent access, such as gorse bushes, can also be grown;
- provide better and clearer warnings.

Falling into deep water and not being able to swim

Options:

- introduce shelving banks - eg one in twelve gradient;
- plant a reed margin;
- install a fence - only if there is no room to change the profile or plant barriers;
- encourage non-swimmers to learn.

Walking on thin ice

- ice tends not to form on moving water;
- avoid creating ponds that are more than one metre deep - bear in mind that reduced depth will benefit some forms of wildlife over others;
- fringe with reeds - reed margins provide a natural barrier to help stop people falling in - as well as helping to entrap pollutants.

A limit to what can be achieved through physical measures

People rarely fall into water without first carrying out some other pre-determining activity. Such activities include walking on thin ice, possibly trying to rescue a dog, drinking or drug taking. Fences alone are unlikely to prevent someone gaining access to a watercourse if they have a mind to do so.

We should ask:

Why did the person fall down the bank?
Why did the person fall into deep water?
Why did the person fall through the ice?
The answers to these questions underline the importance of education and responsible actions when people are near watercourses. For further help see the RoSPA advice documents.

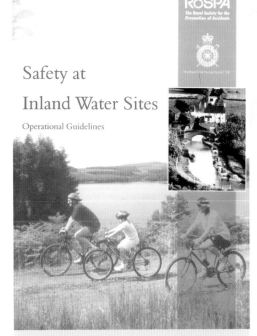

For more advice on water safety contact the Royal Society for the Prevention of Accidents © *RoSPA*

Children are naturally attracted to water. Ensure they are taught to swim and understand the risks. Young children should always be supervised near water. Pond dipping. © *Lorne Gill, SNH*

Ensure hazards are highlighted by using appropriate signage. © *SEPA*

Shopping trolleys and litter lining the river - unfortunately an all too common sight.
© Graham Burns/SCP

A swan nesting on the Clyde amongst the litter.
© Graham Burns/SCP

Step 6 – Actions

Maintenance and monitoring

Litter and refuse

Many open watercourses are used as dumping grounds - collecting rubbish, garden waste, supermarket trolleys, rubble, etc. Litter control on urban watercourses should be to a high standard, or the watercourse will assume an air of dilapidation and neglect that will badly affect how it is perceived by the community. Such litter also increases flooding, if it restricts the waterway.

Riparian owners are sometimes responsible for the maintenance of rivers and Local Authorities have powers to act. Local voluntary groups and communities can help clean up the riverside. However, care needs to be taken to ensure that rubble is not removed from beds which stabilise silty beds, offering shelter for fish and other organisms. There is also a danger of stirring up sediment that may contain toxic components.

Routine maintenance - maintaining the channel

Dredging

Dredging sometimes needs to be carried out when the flow of water becomes obstructed and excessive silt deposition occurs. This process may often be linked to a man-made alteration such as the addition of a culvert. Dredging can be very damaging both to wildlife and the structure of a watercourse. It should be carried out very sensitively once adequate wildlife survey work has been carried out. Clear and very specific instructions should be given to plant operators on what should or should not be done, and where and when.

- Inform SEPA of proposed work prior to commencing and follow appropriate pollution prevention guidance.
- Avoid positioning diggers in the watercourse (although sometimes this is impossible due to reasons of finance or health and safety of workers).
- To limit changes to the river system, dredging work should aim to create a non-uniform channel and should operate from alternating banks to maintain diversity and curvature.
- Avoid pollution from oil and fuels stored nearby.
- Avoid work at times of year that will cause additional stress to wildlife, such as breeding seasons (between October - June for species of migratory fish) etc.
- In light of above, carry out wildlife survey prior to commencing work.

Use of dredged materials

- Ensure dredged materials are used positively and not merely dumped on the edge of the watercourse as pollutants will run-off into the adjacent watercourse.
- Avoid leaving piles of material on bank sides, but allow time for entrapped wildlife to escape prior to removing debris.

Further advice - Environment Agency Guidelines on River Management- SEPA Pollution Prevention Guidance Notes (PPGs) on Works adjacent to watercourses. SEPA should be contacted prior to works being carried out, for advice on pollution avoidance matters.

Weedcutting

Similar care needs to be taken with weedcutting. Weedcutting can devastate invertebrate communities and ruin fisheries by removing large proportions of the food chain on which fish depend. Cut weeds need to be properly disposed of. If they are dumped by the water's edge, bankside vegetation can be damaged, and the liquor from the rotting vegetation can pollute the watercourse. A short period should be left, however, prior to removal to let any animals present in the cuttings escape prior to removal taking place.

Use bankside trees and shrubs to shade the watercourse and restrict weed growth naturally and at no cost.

Ensure weedcutting follows current best practice guidance. Vegetation management guidelines are published (see attached references).

The advantage of low maintenance sustainable drainage systems

Maintenance costs are generally less for Sustainable Urban Drainage Systems (SUDS) than for traditional systems:

- there are no grills to unblock - it can be cheaper to mow a swale (see page 26) than to clean a gully or clear blockages in conventional systems;
- because there are fewer structures to block, flooding is less likely;
- there are no gullies which trap amphibians and need regular de-silting;
- vegetation can be used to reinforce banks, rather than concrete.

The main problems can be administrative. For example, replacing a road edge drain with a swale means that maintenance may be payable from a different budget - gully emptying budget versus grass cutting budget.

Maintaining bankside vegetation - including trees and shrubs

Traditional bankside maintenance can destroy wildlife, reduce the attractiveness of the watercourse, and reduce the potential for the natural stabilisation of the bank by vegetation. Above all, it wastes money.

Control of vegetation can be relatively infrequent. Traditional techniques such as coppicing and pollarding can greatly extend the life-span of trees, enabling the root system to help stabilise the bank. Instead of felling trees to keep the watercourse clear, consider cutting back branches to just above flood level.

A watch should be kept for non-native invasive plants, for example giant hogweed, Japanese knotweed and Indian balsam. If you are unsure about any species, ask the experts and consult literature to be sure. For further advice on control of Japanese knotweed, giant hogweed and other invasive species contact SEPA.

Litter associated with urban water course. © *SEPA*

Guidance is available on the control of alien plant species.
© *Environment Agency*

Benefits to nature, Kingfisher. © *RSPB Images*

Benefits to people and nature. Union Canal, Edinburgh.
© *Derek Braid, Still Moving Picture Company*

The following species highlighted in the Edinburgh Biodiversity Action Plan can be found along rivers and burns:

Animals: water vole, otter, Daubenton's bat, water shrew, pipistrelle bat, kingfisher, swift, reed bunting, sand martin, common toad, river lampery, Atlantic salmon, brown trout, large red damselfly, the cranefly *Tipula gimmerthali*.

Plants: bogbean, flat-stalked pondweed, meadow crane's bill, giant bellflower, hairy stonecrop, water crowfoot, northern yellow-cress.

Extract from The Edinburgh Biodiversity Action Plan. (Rivers and Burns). 2000

5. Make things happen
Check List

- **Recognise the importance of urban watercourses**
  Urban watercourses offer small opportunities, but there are many of them. Cumulatively they amount to a big lost opportunity to enhance quality of life, increase biodiversity and help reverse the decline of urban areas. In encouraging people to live in well designed and habitat friendly urban areas, this may help reduce development in the countryside, reduce dependence on car use, energy consumption, air pollution, and global warming.

- **What do people want?**
  - How do the residents want their neighbourhood to look and to function?
  - What do the local authority want?
  - What do developers want?
  - What do environmental groups or authorities want?
  - Consult the relevant authorities eg local government, environment agencies, and others - obtain their advice. Pre-consultation can make a big difference to the acceptability of a scheme, the quality of advice, degree of support and funding.

- **Develop the idea - what are the problems - what are the options?**
  Undertake a watercourse wildlife and habitat survey to find out what is there, think about different courses of action and the associated problems. Involve professionals to advise on feasibility and best value options, solutions which are self-sustaining and require little or no maintenance etc.

- **Agree a plan** - which could be for the renaissance of a part of the town, including jobs and quality of life, or a more specific plan for greenspace, or a plan entirely related to the watercourse. If there is a riparian or river owner involved, permission to carry out changes has to be obtained from them before any further steps can be taken.

- **Agree a scheme**
- **Find the funds**
- **Implement it**
- **Monitor it**
- **Manage it, Maintain it, Enforce it**

Bear in mind:

- it will take a long time to make changes, but persistence will bring results;
- funding can be found - it makes commercial sense;
- safety concerns can be overcome.

Many local groups are keen to take an active part in protecting their environment. Dighty Environment Group, Dundee. © *SCP, G Burns*

How to form an idea

Forming the Idea

In many areas of life it is a single individual that starts an idea off. The difficulty with urban watercourse projects is that they involve many different groups and individuals. It is important to develop ideas with as many of the groups involved as practicable. Mechanisms may include:

- Focus groups
- Local Area Forums
- Local Agenda 21 process
- Local Biodiversity Action Plans

Sources of Inspiration

- Look at the examples in this guide.
- Visit the SEPA Website:
  www.sepa.org.uk
  SEPA can assist with inquiries, or provide information on many related topics, including - known pollution problems, areas of flood risks and advice on how to avoid pollution whilst carrying out any works adjacent to a watercourse. Information is also available on SEPA's Habitat Enhancement Initiative.
- Contact Scottish Natural Heritage, Scottish Wildlife Trust and local council conservation staff for details of local wildlife designations and conservation groups who may be able to provide information.
- Contact local District Salmon Fishery Boards to establish what the fishery interests may be in the location.
- Visit the Urban Design Alliance Watercourse web site
  www.ice.org.uk/enginfo/watercourses.html
  This includes a listing of schemes already underway, plus further reading.
- Consider usings the UDAL placechecks system to help engage the community and developers. www.placecheck.com
- Contact the River Restoration Centre or visit the web site
  www.qest.demon.co.uk/rrc/rrc.html
- If there is a local flood appraisal group they may also be a useful source of advice.

Persistence

Reversing centuries of neglect may take decades. So it is important to set a long term plan, and to make sure day to day decisions work towards that plan. It is important not to give up.

What do people want?

Consultation and involvement

Consultation should begin at a very early stage, or even used to conceive the project. Consultation takes time.
Consultation needs to establish:

- what local people and business want;
- permission from the land owner;
- the priorities of the agencies involved;
- impressions and perceptions of the possibilities;
- what could and should be done.

The many different people affected by and interested in watercourses will have their own perspective and opinions on what the needs are, and in urban areas these needs can be opposing - at least on the surface.

Habitat Enhancement Initiative © SEPA

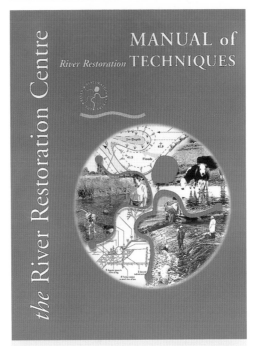

Manual of River Resoration Techniques © RRC

Make things happen

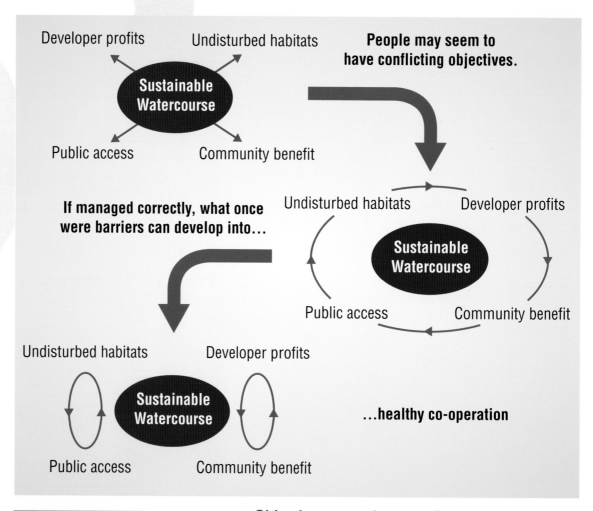

Developer profits   Undisturbed habitats

Sustainable Watercourse

Public access   Community benefit

People may seem to have conflicting objectives.

If managed correctly, what once were barriers can develop into...

Undisturbed habitats   Developer profits

Sustainable Watercourse

Public access   Community benefit

Undisturbed habitats   Developer profits

Sustainable Watercourse

Public access   Community benefit

...healthy co-operation

HABITAT ENHANCEMENT INITIATIVE
DEMONSTRATION SITES & AWARD SCHEME

HEI Demonstration Sites and Award Scheme. © SEPA

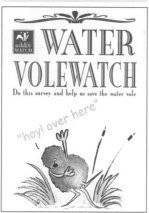

WATER VOLE WATCH

Do this survey and help us save the water vole

"hoy! over here"

Water vole watch © RSNC February 1997. Community groups can have an important input to survey initiatives

Objectives sometimes conflict - with a bit of talking and sensible compromise, everyone can benefit.

The consultation process needs to include an element of education - people generally do not understand fluvial geomorphology. They may even think that a channellised watercourse is a sewer. Sometimes it is! Local people may well have better local knowledge than professionals.

Working with the community

Local community groups (recommended under the Local Agenda 21 process) can be used.

The Local Agenda 21 process promotes a number of areas for local sustainability including:

- listening to what people want and involve them in making decisions which affect them;
- increasing access to local facilities;
- building on local strengths and try to add value locally;
- increasing the opportunities for local employment, education and training;
- strengthening the local community and cultural identity.

Many improvements to watercourses can be carried out with the help of local volunteers, either from the community generally or by special interest groups and educational establishments. They can also be incorporated into 'welfare to work' and other similar schemes.

Public attitude

People generally view water very positively, but are rarely aware of the possibilities for river restoration and improvement within their own town. Past research shows that they receive proposals for restoration enthusiastically - often over 80 percent are in favour. In contrast there can be opposition to schemes involving hard engineering.

Develop the idea

See section 4. Working with Water.

Role for the professional

Before any work is undertaken it is important to understand the catchment and the ecology of the watercourse.
The final design will need to blend the differing viewpoints of local interests with the practical requirements of the numerous local authority departments likely to be involved in the implementation and subsequent maintenance of the scheme.

Many techniques need professional design - for example, meander shape, riffle spacings and design. It is important to work with the river's natural dynamics to avoid mistakes that would be costly and damaging or only be short-term features requiring maintenance. Contact the River Restoration Centre as a source of information.

Funding can be found

Lack of finance is often cited as the reason for ignoring our watercourses, yet there are many potential sources of funds available to help with such schemes.

Restoring watercourses makes sense in hard cash terms - it increases the value of surrounding development substantially and in the long-term, reduces maintenance costs.

There are numerous other sources of funds - for the greatest likelihood of funding try to develop a scheme package which can tap into a number of different budgets - such as environmental, regeneration, social exclusion, and the local transport plan: a well conceived scheme will bring in a wide range of benefits. Individual sources include:

- developers
- local authorities
- environmental trusts
- Scottish Executive
- Scottish Enterprise
- Highlands & Islands Enterprise
- environmental bodies dispensing landfill tax funding
- local business
- trusts set up to promote the environment
- lottery funds
- Scottish Natural Heritage
- European Union - especially the EU LIFE programme
- Scottish Environment Protection Agency limited funding of demonstration sites.

With a little research into the most appropriate source, and a partnership approach between the public and private sector, funding should not be an insurmountable problem. Above all, long term maintenance of the completed scheme must be funded.

Hierarchy for the improvement of urban watercourses

Objective 1 - reduce flood risk - use natural, sustainable drainage measures - all catchments

Objective 2 - enhance the natural habitat - all watercourses

- make sure the watercourse acts as a wildlife corridor - and does not obstruct wildlife;
- provide habitat for wildlife;
- ensure environmental damage is avoided - contact SNH to see if there are wildlife designations, contact council to establish if there are relevant Local Biodiversity Action plans in the area, contact SEPA for information about avoiding pollution, fisheries trusts for fisheries information, etc;
- prevent pollution from entering the watercourse.

Objective 3 - enhance the human habitat - most watercourses

- make sure the watercourse can be enjoyed by citizens - as something to look at, to walk, cycle or to sit beside.

Objective 4 - enhance the built environment - most urban areas (long term)

- make sure development respects and benefits from, the watercourse.

Before... River Skerne prior to fitting of revetments (view looking upstream). © *RRC*

After...River Skerne revetments fitted (Type A deflector) vegetation established (view looking downseam). © *RRC*

The significance of historic features in a watercourse can be revealed by a survey.

Breadalbane Folklore Centre. © SEPA

Biological survey. © SEPA

Rivers are used for a number of recreation purposes, such as fishing. © Lorne Gill, SNH

Actions for Local Authorities

Local authorities are in the key position to bring about change: involving the community and seeking their views and advice, working within the Local Agenda 21 process, working with developers and much more.

Councillors

Champion the restoration of the watercourses in your town:
- as one of the best options for improving wildlife habitats and corridors;
- as a component of a network of new pedestrian and cycle routes;
- as potentially the most attractive parts of the town - improving people's quality of life and attracting inward investment, as a recreation and amenity resource.

Key thoughts...

- allocate additional resources to watercourse restoration and maintenance in its own right;
- have restoration of urban watercourses as an integral part of policies on social exclusion, urban regeneration, and sustainable transport;
- act as advocate for a better town - broker partnerships between the many different organisations that need to be brought together to bring it about.

Watercourse survey

Ideally a local authority's policy on its watercourses should be guided by a survey of existing watercourses and other water features, including their past, and present uses. The end product is not a survey but a restored watercourse, so the survey should be as long as necessary to provide useful guidance on how to go about restoring the watercourse and no longer than that.
Coverage should include
- the general nature and characteristics of the watercourse;
- the existing range of habitats and biodiversity;
- historic use of watercourses, eg. archaeology, disused or lost mills, millponds, lades and tail-races, wharves, monastic fishponds, moats, etc., and the possibility for restoration;
- how the watercourse is currently used;
- identification of any other plans or policies that could provide guidance, eg proposals in local plan etc.

Local people will often be a valuable source of advice, and the expertise and enthusiasm available in organisations such as SNH and SEPA and relevant charities and trusts should be sought.
The survey should be used to identify opportunities to:
- protect existing habitats and biodiversity interests of note;
- remove any barriers to the movement of wildlife up and down the watercourse, and the possibility for creating wildlife corridors;
- provide new habitats and a more natural appearance;
- provide access for the public;
- incorporate watercourse corridors into a wider footpath or cycle path network.
Again the views of the community and of specialist organisations should be sought in helping to identify opportunities.

A watercourse map can be developed - analogous to the public rights of way map, with policies on future development and habitat protection and enhancement related to each watercourse. These surveys are a valuable and additional activity, requiring additional funding and staff resources. See section on funding in chapter 5 Make things happen.

Structure plans

Should include:
- a general policy on how watercourses within the area are to contribute to economic, leisure and amenity activities, habitat and public rights of way;
- advice that local plans should presume against development within the floodplain;
- a requirement that the impact of development should be assessed throughout an entire catchment;
- policies on the use of sustainable urban drainage techniques in new developments.

Local plans

Should include: general policies:
- a presumption against placing watercourses in culverts. (See SEPA's policy on culverting - see appendix for summary);
- a statement on the value of restoring urban watercourses for nature, community, commercial and urban regeneration interest;
- a policy to enhance and restore watercourses in re-developments (i.e. the breaking out, or daylighting, of culverts) should be encouraged;
- a policy to protect urban watercourses which are in a natural state;
- a policy to restrict development immediately next to, or over, urban watercourses, where this would prejudice the creation of a future public right of way or wildlife corridor.

Policies relating to types of area:
- residential areas - where a watercourse can be a valuable leisure facility, and where a new public right of way along the watercourse can play its part in creating a larger network of footpaths or cycleways connecting with other parts of the town;
- industrial areas - where watercourses can contribute to the general improvement of the environment, but are especially at risk from pollution;
- town centres - where water features can form an important attraction for town centre users.

Specific policies relating to individual watercourses of particular importance and potential:
- how the watercourse should be included in, and protected from, new developments, and Sustainable Urban Drainage techniques included.

Development design guidance

Development design guidance should be extended to cover urban watercourse matters, including the use of sustainable urban drainage techniques.

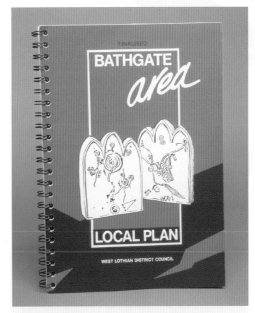

One way to help ensure sustainable development policies are followed is through their inclusion in relevant structure and local plans. Bathgate Local Plan Photograph. © SEPA

Carryout pre-development survey work to ensure that existing aquatic habitats and species are protected. A valued water feature. © CIBIA

Take opportunities to incorporate habitat issues positively when seeking advice from other bodies and agencies. SEPA Planning Liaison Officer. © SEPA

The River Clyde running through the centre of Glasgow. © P A Macdonald, SNH

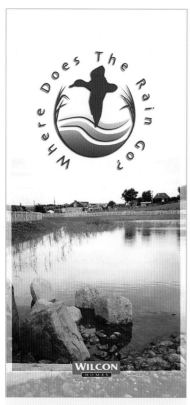

Design guidance. Education is an important part of the process. © Wilcon Homes

Guidance may include advice that:

- SEPA and SNH should be consulted at an early stage
- Habitat and species surveys, should be undertaken before plans are prepared.
- Watercourses should be left unchanged if their habitat quality is good, otherwise physical modifications may be needed to change flow patterns. If not carried out carefully there may be a risk of erosion, siltation and increased flooding further downstream.
- Development should not be encouraged on the flood plain.
- Having taken consideration of the above point, development should incorporate the watercourses as a positive aspect creating a clear identity for the development, greater attractiveness, and potentially greater value. Ideally, development should face the watercourse rather than access roads.
- Safety measures should be considered where necessary, such as grading back artificially steepened banks to improve public access and safety and increase flood protection potential. However safety should not be taken to a phobic extreme that sees the watercourse sterilised and isolated. It is safe behaviour that is particularly important.
- Public rights of way along watercourses should be considered with a view towards linking adjoining sites. However, their design needs to be in keeping with the watercourse and a balance should be struck with the natural habitat. Sometimes, walkways should be run down just one side of the river to leave the other as a haven for wildlife.
- Channellised watercourses can be restored through reintroducing natural features such as pools and riffles etc., to increase visual amenity, form new habitats, and to increase flood protection potential.
- Hard engineering measures, such as concrete faced outlets and walls, should be avoided and soft engineering alternatives should be used in preference, eg stabilisation of banks using vegetation.
- Appropriate landscaping should be provided, with a natural emphasis including trees to provide shading and control vegetation within the watercourse.
- Opportunities to integrate habitat enhancement and public recreation, including angling, be sought and promoted.

Development control

- Ensure all new major developments incorporate a Sustainable Urban Drainage approach - minimise the area of impermeable surfaces created in new developments by careful attention to site layout, minimising pavement and tarmac space, minimise the area of impermeable surfaces.
- Ensure plans for the treatment of watercourses and drainage on the site are submitted at the same time, and preferably as part of the detailed planning application. Insist that the plans mark the watercourses and proposed treatments.
- Check that the promoters have obtained advice on flood risk, and have assessed the habitats and species in and around the site and watercourses. Ensure wildlife suvey results are included.
- Resist development which contravenes SEPA policies on culverting.
- Encourage the developer to realise the potential of the positive use of watercourses as part of a high quality design.

- Ensure no structures restrict free passage of fish up and downstream.
- Ensure pollution is tackled at source before entering the drainage system.

Monitoring and maintenance

A natural watercourse can be among the most attractive features in a town, but unless it is well monitored and maintained it can become an advert for urban decay.

- Set high standards of maintenance, including litter control, and adhere to them. Encourage local communities (for example using the Local Agenda 21 process) to take an interest in the husbandry of their watercourses.
- Ensure the landscaping is designed with maintenance in mind and that funding for future maintenance is safeguarded.
- Where possible, secure long-term funding for the monitoring and maintenance of a watercourse from developers by commuted sum, bonds or other means.

If properly monitored and maintained rivers and burns can become sanctuaries for nature. Heron. © K Ringland

Actions for developers

- Specify sustainable urban drainage systems.
- Consider the benefit to your company of demonstrating its environmental policy in practice.
- Contact SEPA for further advice.

Sites with watercourses - no matter how small.

- Remember that the presence of burns or open water can increase the value of developments.

Checklist

Does it flood?	Consult: • local authorities, especially planning and conservation departments • other regulatory bodies, eg SEPA • local people • local flood appraisal groups - where in existence • seek advice from hydro-geomorphologists	• Yes	**Used land** - Re-assess flood protection methods. Think about designing around the flood risk to avoid the need for flood protection measures - eg can a car park be allowed to flood? **New land** - think about finding a new site. If land next to the watercourse floods, then do not develop the site.
		• No	Move to next step
Does a watercourse flow through, next to, or underneath the site?	Consult: • Local Authority • SEPA	• Yes	**Used land** - enhance what is there already. If the watercourse has been heavily modified see if it is possible to restore it to a more natural form. **New land** - Obtain professional advice on how best to realise the potential water has on the site to increase its final value. If the watercourse is in a natural state, keep it that way. Leave a margin around the watercourse.
		• No	Remember that there may be culverted steams and surface water drains not immediatly apparent - take all resonable steps to identify these
Is there information on what is on the site?	Consult: • SEPA • Local Authority including planning and conservation departments • other regulatory bodies, eg SNH • non government organisations such as Scottish Wildlife Trust (SWT), Royal Society for the Protection of Birds (RSPB) • local people, fisheries trusts • existing research	• Yes	Normally, designs can be produced that incorporate the habitat into the development - in such a way that any protected species is safeguarded from disturbance.
		• No	Commission a habitat survey - SNH and SEPA can provide advice. It is best to find this out before designs are produced. If it is at the construction stage that a protected habitat or species is discovered, the consequences can be very expensive. It is better to find out what is there right from the start. The presence of a protected species on-site does not mean financial ruin.

Actions

Identify ways to protect and, where relevant, improve habitats	→	Obtain advice on protecting and enhancing habitats from SNH, Local Authority conservation staff, River Restoration Centre and SEPA.
What about water quality, fisheries, ecology?	→	Obtain advice on pollution prevention from SEPA, and fisheries interests from District Salmon Fishery Boards and SNH.
What are the surroundings like?	→	Make use of the natural topography of the site: not only the watercourse, but also slopes and existing trees.
Think about design and aesthetics	→	Create a layout for buildings which creates attractive spaces, and incorporates the watercourse as a central feature. Do not create a layout which turns its back on the watercourse - the consequence can be a dead area, prone to collect litter and refuse, which is seen as a blight on the development. Do not culvert existing watercourses. If possible, open up existing culverts to create aesthetically pleasing landscapes.
Think about access and roads	→	Work in the road layout around the buildings, checking for minimum clearances and turning radii.
Remember...	→	Use sustainable urban drainage techniques and soft engineering! Design advice is now available.

The end product can be a plan for a highly attractive development which will have a greater chance of obtaining planning permission and which will command higher prices, as well as meeting environmental objectives.

Points to watch

- Site plans that seek to eliminate watercourses are likely to encounter significant opposition from local authorities, SEPA and SNH.
- If the watercourse is already culverted up or down stream then the arguments for retaining the watercourse in its natural state become even stronger, as do the financial returns for producing a distinctive development.
- Blocking and in-filling watercourses may result in flooding, and prosecution.
- Culverted watercourses tend to become blocked and result in flooding of adjoining properties. The developer may be it risk of legal action by owners of adjoining property. Work on the site which damages habitats or species may lead to prosecution.

Actions for engineers

Take a leading role by showing how watercourses could be protected and restored and emphasise the resulting benefits. Keep abreast of developing advice on more sustainable options.

Philosophy on interference with burns and rivers

Rivers naturally adjust their channel dimensions to the flow transporting the most sediment. This flow is equivalent to the bankfull flow of the natural channel. As a rough guide, the bankfull flow or channel forming flow will occur every one to two years. If the channel dimensions are made artificially smaller or larger than those created by the watercourse's sediment and flow regime, the river will try to fight back and regain its regime dimensions.

- In over widened channels, this means deposition of sediment and the need for on-going maintenance. In over deepened channels, there is tendency for the artificially high banks to collapse and help decrease the depth of the river again.
- Straightening a watercourse increases another important dimension, its gradient. The increase in energy of a steepened reach allows the destabilised watercourse to transport more sediment, which it is hungry to strip from its bed and banks and then deposit it downstream.

Nature knows best in determining the most stable river form.

Philosophy on drainage

- Use sustainable urban drainage techniques on all new developments to reduce run-off and intercept pollution.
- Use soft engineering techniques wherever possible.
- Use your skill and expertise to bring out the full potential benefit of the watercourse.

Are there any drainage or habitat issues?	→	Consult • SEPA and SNH. • local authorities in development control matters initiatives, flood control etc.
Restoration	→	• Incorporate restoration measures wherever possible as an integral part of capital works on degraded rivers. If opportunities are sought from the start, implementing them may not make the scheme any more expensive, and may lead to a cheaper design. • Promote the restoration of a river where appropriate to a more natural state - see the sections in the guide and the references provided.
Environment	→	• Avoid damage to the river bed, banks, and the habitats they provide. • Avoid changing watercourses in a way that will damage habitats, change sediment deposition or erosion rates. • Consult SEPA for advice on pollution prevention guidance during civil engineering works.
Understanding	→	Aim to use the understanding of natural river processes to reduce the need for maintenance. Remember - rivers naturally adjust
Monitoring and maintenance	→	Ensure adequate monitoring survey work is carried out and maintenance is sympathetic to the river form and its habitats
If you think it is better to place a watercourse in a culvert...	→	• Check with SEPA against its policy on culverts. • Check with authorities on fisheries about potentially blocking fish passage. • Establish the consequences of a blockage in the culvert. • Compare the costs of ongoing maintenance of a culvert, versus the cost of a swale or other alternative. • See if there are alternatives.
Funding	→	Do not be despondent if there is insufficient funding to do the job you would like to do - demonstrate to your clients, via business cases and cost/benefits of various options.

Actions for communities

Watercourses can form a key part of your community, increasing the quality of life for all.

Enjoy your local burn or river	→	Encourage education and awareness of, and respect for, watercourses, their wildlife and their history.
Improve your local environment	→	Work with your local authority in developing schemes for restoring the watercourse and improving your local environment.
Sustainable drainage	→	• Avoid washing cars, etc, on the road, or tipping oil or wheelie bin washings into gullypots, as the waste may drain straight into the nearest river. Alternatively go to a car wash, or wash the vehicle or wheelie bin on a permeable surface, etc. * • if you are creating hard standing for your car, make sure it drains into a soakaway or is made of permeable material, such as gravel.
Safety	→	Consider the safety aspects during the early stages of the project and ensure they are worked into the final design.
Involvement	→	• Organise litter clear-up days in association with your local authority and/or SEPA to immediately improve the appearance of your watercourse. **NB** Check with Local Authority or SEPA that it is safe first.

* Some wheelie bin washers have contained recirculation units that do not discharge wastes to the environment. Always check what system is used.

Action for individuals living next to watercourses

Have you made the most of your watercourse?	Consider: • is it an asset? • is it unconfined? • does it look healthy? • is it a feature?	• Yes • No	Enjoy the watercourse! • Avoid blocking off the views to the watercourse with high fences or walls. • Keep the banks natural. If you need to reinforce them, use natural products and/or vegetation.
Are you responsible for the maintenance of the river bank?	Maintenance of a river bank lies in the first instance with the riparian owner	• Yes • No	**Excellent** - keep enjoying the benefits! • Consult appropriate bodies about maintenance regimes and practices. • Create a programme that is achievable and right for you.
Are there precautions against accidental pollution?	Consider the risks: • look around at what could enter the watercourse • oil, compost run-off, etc.	• Yes • No	• Excellent! Encourage others to follow your example. • Consult appropriate bodies. • Do not store diesel or other polluting materials adjacent to a watercourse, these sorts of spills can cause massive damage to a watercourse, and result in large fines.
Are you careful?	Consider the little things		• Do not dispose of refuse, including garden waste, in the watercourse or on the riverbank. • Do not dispose of waste such as oils and paints from maintenance or decorating or wheelie bin and car washings into rivers or roadside gully pots. The latter may be directly connected to the nearest burn - take waste materials to the recycling centre or disposable site. If your road drains connect to the nearest burn, ensure you either take your car to the car wash or wash it on a permeable surface.

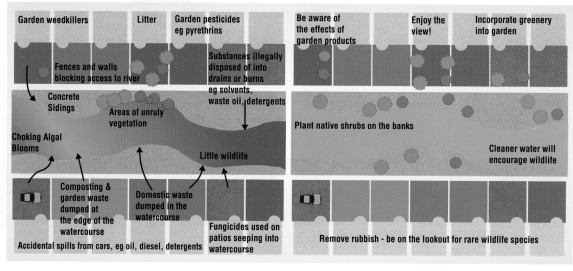

Unsustainable (BAD) River Care

Garden weedkillers | Litter | Garden pesticides eg pyrethrins

Fences and walls blocking access to river

Substances illegally disposed of into drains or burns eg solvents, waste oil, detergents

Concrete Sidings

Areas of unruly vegetation

Choking Algal Blooms

Little wildlife

Composting & garden waste dumped at the edge of the watercourse

Domestic waste dumped in the watercourse

Fungicides used on patios seeping into watercourse

Accidental spills from cars, eg oil, diesel, detergents

Sustainable (GOOD) River Care

Be aware of the effects of garden products | Enjoy the view! | Incorporate greenery into garden

Plant native shrubs on the banks

Cleaner water will encourage wildlife

Remove rubbish - be on the lookout for rare wildlife species

Actions for parents

Can your child swim?	Yes	Warn children they should not walk on ice or swim in rivers and ponds, and certainly never when unaccompanied.
	No	Enrol them in swimming lessons.
Do you teach your child to appreciate the beauty and danger of rivers and ponds?	Yes	Well done, hopefully they will be more likely to appreciate the natural beauty of their surroundings, tell friends and enjoy a safe and shared experience
	No	• Use the watercourse as a doorway to improve your child's understanding of nature and the environment. • Seek advice from RoSPA on water safety.

Kids playing in a burn at Little Glenshee - Simple pleasures. © *Lorne Gill, SNH* (NB Young children should always be supervised near water).

7. Information and Advice

The information included in this section, and in the document generally, is for general guidance only and does not represent detailed legal advice. If you require further clarification of legal issues, please contact your solicitor for further advice.

Responsibilities for urban watercourses and drainage

Responsibility for river maintenance may rest with local authorities and the riparian owners, so that any change in the maintenance regime may need their commitment and co-operation.

Many of the responsibilities described below are not statutory duties, but are actions and policies which contribute to sustainable development - most organisations mentioned have responsibilities towards this. The quantity and quality of water is significant for aquatic habitats and species. SNH, SEPA and other organisations often liaise closely to deliver conservation objectives for watercourses.

Water quality

- Point source discharges - SEPA regulates (issues consents, monitors compliance).
- Surface water run-off from curtilage drainage - SEPA, Water Authority and local authority planners promote use of SUDS in new developments through planning consultation process (and encourage retrospective fitting where specific problems identified). SEPA investigates pollution incidents, provides guidance on pollution prevention.
- Surface water run-off from road drainage - SEPA, Water Authority and local authority planners and roads engineers promote use of SUDS in new road developments through planning consultation process (and encourage retrospective fitting where specific problems identified). SEPA investigates pollution incidents, provides guidance on pollution prevention.

Water quantity

- Monitored by SEPA - rivers and groundwater.
- Abstraction licences - may be required in areas designated by statute and are required where rivers are vulnerable to over-abstraction. In most other areas abstraction is not controlled.
- SEPA operates flood warning systems in some parts of Scotland (though not a statutory duty).
- Promotion of SUDS through planning consultation process may help abate flash flooding due to run-off (SEPA / local authorities - in urban areas and wider catchment area).
- SEPA provides advice on flood risk via planning consultation process.

Development

Local Authorities are committed to formulating a Local Agenda 21 Strategy, and already take into account sustainable development issues when developing Local Plans.

- The planning process can:
  - use powers to promote river restoration and enhancement;
  - prevent development on flood plains;
  - promote use of SUDS;
  - encourage 'water sensitive' development.
- SEPA and SNH should be consulted on planning applications as above and may generally promote sustainability issues to engineers/developers etc such as SUDS, HEI.

Flood defence and alleviation

Primary responsibility for flood defence rests with landowners, and erosion control with the riparian owner. Local Authorities have permissive powers, measures they consider necessary, to prevent and mitigate flooding of non agricultural land if deemed to be in the public interest. Under Flood Prevention (Scotland) Act 1961, as amended by the Flood Prevention and Land Drainage (Scotland) Act 1997.

- SEPA, SNH, WWF, SWT etc promote the nature conservation value of specific watercourses and promote soft engineering techniques where applicable.
- SEPA provides advice on flood risk via planning process.
- SEPA and SNH participate in Flood Appraisal Groups.

River maintenance and management

- Local authorities and riparian owners may be responsible for management (dredging, weedcutting etc).
- Promotion of less intrusive or intensive maintenance routines where appropriate (LA, SEPA, SNH).
- Local authorities and riparian owners may be responsible for litter removal, removal of obstructions etc.

Responsibilities for urban watercourses and wildlife

Biodiversity and wildlife

- Government via LBAP Partnerships, generally lead by local authorities, but including SNH, SEPA, etc responsible for contributing to protection and enhancement of biodiversity through mechanisms such as Local Biodiversity Action Plans (LBAPs - not obligatory, but a mechanism for local authorities to fulfil wider obligations with regard to Local Agenda 21 and Sustainable Development), and Habitat Enhancement Initiative (SEPA).

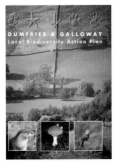

Local Biodiversity Action Plans

Local Biodiversity Action Plan - a process which aims to ensure that nationally and locally important habitats and species are conserved and enhanced through locally, focused action. LBAPs are initiated and implemented by biodiversity partnerships and most councils now have, or are preparing, them. They aim to produce practical solutions to improve the local environment, and increase community awareness - many LBAPs consider rivers and burns.

Natura 2000/SSSI network

Throughout Europe, a network of protected areas for wildlife are being set up to protect our most precious habitats and species - this will build upon the existing network of Sites of Special Scientific Interest. There are currently five rivers in Scotland that are protected as part of the Natura 2000/SSSI network.

Wildlife Sites

Wildlife sites recognised by the Scottish Wildlife Trust usually do not have statutory designated protection, but have been recognised for their intrinsic wildlife value. There are many wildlife sites in Scotland; some are on or incorporate rivers and burns. These sites are non-statutory, but many are recognised in local authority Local Plans and therefore protected from development.

Local Nature Reserves (LNR)

Local Authorities can select and designate Local Nature Reserves. Ideally they will be situated in close proximity to the communities in the area, with the aim of providing people with the opportunity to learn about, study, or simply enjoy the wildlife on their doorstep. There are numerous LNR's, including Arnhall Moss in Gordon and Donmouth in Aberdeen, and more are planned for the future.

National Planning Policy Guideline 14 - Natural Heritage

Government advises that local authorities should take particular care to avoid harm to species or habitats protected under the 1981 wildlife and countryside Act, European Directives or identified as priorities in the UK Biodiversity Action Plan.

Rivers and burns that don't have rare species, or are not protected as wildlife sites, are still important and can contribute a great deal to biodiversity. They also act as wildlife corridors, and are a refuge for wildlife and humans from built-up areas.

Organisations (Contact details)

CIRIA - has produced a number of research projects on sustainable urban drainage. Tel: 020 7222 8891 Fax: 020 7222 1708

ICE - is actively campaigning as part of the Urban Design Alliance for the enhancement of urban watercourses and urban areas in general. Tel: 020 7222 7722 Fax: 020 7222 7500 Website: www.ice.org.uk

Local Authorities - There are 32 councils in Scotland serving the needs of local communities. All are involved in planning and are an important point of call when considering a community based river restoration project. Contact details for your nearest local authority are available in the local phone book.

River Restoration Centre - an independent UK organisation, supported by SNH and SEPA in Scotland, which provides advice on river rehabilitation. It has produced leaflets, a manual of techniques and film of demonstration sites and has a database detailing examples of hundreds of restoration projects. Tel: 01525 863341 Fax: 01525 863341 website: www.quest.demon.co.uk/rrc/rrc.htm

SEPA - Scottish Environment Protection Agency - has produced a range of policies and guidance on river restoration and management. SEPA has developed the Habitat Enhancement Initiative with the following mission statement - *'Through its own actions and in conjunction with external partners, SEPA will advise and influence target sectors to help secure measurable improvement in the way in which habitats are managed. In particular SEPA will focus on the aquatic and riparian habitats and the conservation and enhancement of biodiversity interests, under the power of the Environment Act (1995), section 34.* (Contact details for SEPA inside of back cover).

The Freshwaters Fisheries Laboratory - gives advice on all aspects of fish conservation and protection. For further information contact Tel: 01796 472060 Fax: 01796 473523

Scottish Executive Rural Affairs Department (Fisheries Group). Gives advice on fisheries legislation which has to be taken into consideration during river works Tel: 0131 244 6231 Fax: 0131 244 6313

SNH - Scottish Natural Heritage - the statutory nature conservation agency in Scotland, provides advice to government, promotes sustainable development of the natural heritage, and promotes and enhances the conservation of wildlife and natural features (including geology, geomorphology and landscape) across all areas of Scotland. SNH also has a recreational role. Tel: 0131 447 4784 Fax: 0131 446 2405

SWT - Scottish Wildlife Trust - is the largest of the 46 regional Wildlife Trusts and 52 Urban Wildlife Trusts which make up The Wildlife Trusts partnership. The Wildlife Trusts partnership cares for over 2,300 wildlife reserves UK-wide, and works to protect and conserve the UK's wildlife and wild places. Tel: 0131 312 7765 Fax: 0131 312 8705

WWF - World Wide Fund for Nature - the world's largest independent conservation organisation. It operates on a global scale through 27 National Organisations and commands support well into the millions. It compiles and supplies information on a wide range of issues. Tel: 01887 820449 Fax: 01887 829453

Water and Nature

GUIDANCE

Environmental Assessment and Scoping Studies
EU water quality directives
Fisheries
Habitat Plans
Local Biodiversity Action Plans
Proposed Water Framework Directive
Species Plans
UK Biodiversity Action Plan

REFERENCES

Nature Conservation and River Engineering - C Newbold, J Purseglove, N Holmes. Nature Conservancy Council. Peterborough. 1983.

Urban Rivers: Nature Conservation and the Use of Rivers for Recreation - Eds: Hall & Smith. Riverbank Conservation. University of Hertfordshire. 1991.

The New Rivers & Wildlife Handbook - RSPB, NRA & RSNC. 1994. ISBN 0 903138 70 0

The Edinburgh Biodiversity Action Plan - The Edinburgh Biodiversity Partnership. March 2000.

Engineering the Creation of Wildlife Habitats in the River - Alt and Maghull Brook. Ian Rowlands. CIWEM Rivers & Coastal Group/ Environment Group. 31 January 1997.

Environmental Guidelines for Vegetation Management in Channel & on banks - Environment Agency. River Maintenance evaluation phase 3. R&D Project W5A-048. Also associated reports W134 - The evaluation of FDMM, and W135.

River Crossings and Migratory Fish: Design Guidance: Consultation Paper - Scottish Executive. April 2000

Water Vole Conservation Handbook - Environment Agency et al. 1998. ISBN 09529 3715

Water and People

Reference

Urban Rivers: Nature Conservation and the Use of Rivers for Recreation - Eds: Hall & Smith. Riverbank Conservation. University of Hertfordshire. 1991.

Water and the Built Environment

GUIDANCE

NPPG 7 Planning and Flooding etc

References

Environmental Good Practice Guide for the Development of Urban, Industrial and Commercial Sites - Environment Agency, Groundwork (Birmingham), Ove Arup & Partners, Severn Trent Water plc. July 1998.

Review of the design and management of constructed wetlands - R180 CIRIA.

The Millennium Riverbank Experience - Greenwich Means Time for a new Outlook on Riverside Development - Environment Agency August. 1997.

Working with Water

Catchments

Applied Fluvial Geomorphology for River Engineering and Management - Ed. C R Thorne, R D Hey, & M D Newson. Wiley and Sons.

Taming the Flood - A History and Natural History of Rivers and Wetlands - J Purseglove. OUP in association with Channel Four Television Company. 1988.

River Habitat Quality - Raven, PG, Holmes, NTH, Dawson, FH, Fox, PTA, Everard, M, Fozzard, IR & Rouen, KJ. 1998. ISBN 1-873160-429

Nature Conservation and the Management of Drainage Channels - C Newbold, J Hannar & K Buckley. English Nature. 1989.

Engineering Methods for Scottish Gravel Bed Rivers. SNH review number 47. Hoey, TB, et al. 1998.

Ponds, Pools and Lochans. Guidance on good practice in the management and creation of small waterbodies in Scotland. SEPA June 2000 - ISBN 1-901322-16-5

Other Sources
SEPA Website - Permeate On-line
www.sepa.org.uk/guidance/control/permeate.htm
SEPA Policy 26 - Culverting of Watercourses.

Sustainable Urban Drainage

Infiltration Drainage - Case Studies of Good Practice - CIRIA PR22. Prof C J Pratt. 1992.

Design of Flood Storage Reservoirs - Hall, Hockin, Ellis, Butterworth, & Heinemann. 1993.

Urban Drainage - The Natural Way - Hydro Research & Development Ltd. (Tel: 01275 878371) 1993.

Infiltration Drainage - Appraisal of Costs - CIRIA PR24. Roberts. 1995.

Infiltration Drainage - Legal Aspects - CIRIA PR25 Prof. W Howarth & A. Brierley. 1995.

Infiltration Drainage - Literature Review - CIRIA PR21. D.Watkins. 1995.

Infiltration Drainage - Hydraulic Design - CIRIA PR23. Bettes, Davis, & Watkins. 1996.

Infiltration Drainage - Manual of Good Practice - CIRIA Report 156. R. Bettes. 1996.

Protecting the Quality of Our Environment - A Guide to Sustainable Urban Drainage - Scottish Environment Protection Agency & Environment Agency. September 1997.

Searching for Sustainability - source control of surface water run-off from development - B. Winter. Proc 32nd MAFF Conference of River and Coastal Engineers. 1997.

Sustainable Urban Water Management - Notes of a Construction Industry Environmental Forum (CIEF) Workshop. 8 July 1997. (Available from CIRIA).

Design of reinforced grass waterways - R116 CIRIA.

Nature's Way - (Video). International Association on Water Quality et al.

Proceedings of the Standing Committee on Storm Water Source Control - Prof. C J Pratt; School of the Built Environment. Coventry University.

Scope for Control of Urban Run-off - CIRIA Report 123/4., Vols. 1-4. Ed. Marshall, Sherriff, Leonard.

Sustainable Urban Drainage Systems Design Manual for Scotland and Northern Ireland - CIRIA C521, CIRIA and Substainable Urban Drainage Working Party, March 2000. ISBN 0 86017 5219

Sustainable Urban Drainage Systems: Setting the Scene in Scotland - SEPA. June 2000.

Urban Drainage - A European Environmental Perspective - Techware CSO Information Group.

Soft engineering and Watercourse Restoration

References

Waterside Planning Design Handbook - British Waterways. 1996.

Design Imperatives for River Landscapes - O D Manning. Landscape Research. Vol 22, No 1. March 1997. pp67-94.

Promoting River Restoration in the UK - The River Restoration Centre. 1997.

Engineering methods for Scottish gravel bed rivers - Hoey, T.B., Smart, D.J.W., Pender, G. and Metcalfe, N. (Edited by Leys, K.) 1998. Scottish Natural Heritage Review No 47

Channellised Rivers: Perspectives for Environmental Management - Andrew Brookes, John Wiley & Sons. 1998.

Revetment techniques used on the River Skerne restoration project - Environment Agency R&D Technical Report W83. WRc 1998.

Waterway bank protection: a guide to erosion assessment and management - Environment Agency R&D Project W5-635. Cranfield University. 1999.

Manual of River Restoration Techniques - River Restoration Centre, Cranfield, Beds. 1999.

Riverbank Protection using Willow -Environment Agency Scoping Study W5A011. University of Nottingham.

Planning

GUIDANCE

NPPG7 - Planning and Flooding
NPPG14 - Natural Heritage
Flood Risk Assessment
SEPA Policy 22 Flood Risk Assessment Strategy
Flood appraisal groups
Local Authority
Structure Plan
Local Plan

References

Design Imperatives for River Landscapes - O D Manning. Landscape Research. Vol 22, No 1. March 1997. pp67-94.

Partnership in Planning - Riverbank Design Guidance for the Tidal Thames - Environment Agency. March 1997.

Policy, Law and Regulations

1950

Rivers (Prevention of Pollution) (Scotland) Act 1951
Salmon and Freshwater (Protection) (Scotland) Act 1951

1960

Rivers (Prevention of Pollution) (Scotland) Act 1965
Flood prevention (Scotland) Act 1961, as amended by the Flood Prevention and Land Drainage (Scotland) Act 1997

1970

Control of Pollution Act 1974
Salmon and Freshwater Fisheries Act 1975
EC Directive on the Conservation of Wild Birds (Directive 79/409/EEC)

1980

Wildlife and Countryside Act 1981
Salmon Act 1986
Control of Pollution (Amendment) Act 1989
Water Act 1989

1990

Environmental Protection Act 1990
Town and Country Planning Act 1990
Natural Heritage (Scotland) Act 1991
Wildlife and Countryside (Amendment) Act 1991
EC Directive on the Conservation of Natural Habitats and of Wild Flora and Fauna (Directive 92/43/EEC)
Conservation (Natural Habitats etc) Regulations 1994
The Salmon (Fish Passes & Screens) (Scotland) regulations 1994
UK Biodiversity Action Plan. 1994.
Environment Act 1995
Scottish Office Circular 6/1995, Habitats and Birds Directives
National Planning Policy Guidance 14 - Natural Heritage.

International

Ramsar Convention - Wetlands of International Importance (especially waterfowl habitats)
Berne Convention - the Conservation of European Wildlife and Natural Habitats

Funding

Single sources

Developers
Local Authorities
Scottish Executive
Environmental charities
Local Business
Landfill tax

Package type funding

Where watercourse restoration aims to achieve several goals e.g. - urban regeneration, transport plans

Consultation and Community

GUIDANCE

Modernising Local Government
Local Government Management Board guidance on Local Agenda 21 process

REFERENCES

DETR - Sustainable Local Communities for the 21st Century. A Guide for local authorities to the implementation of Agenda 21 strategies - HMSO. 1998.

8. Glossary

Agenda 21 - A non-binding comprehensive framework for world-wide action, based on 13 environmentally related themes:

- agriculture,
- atmosphere,
- biological diversity,
- biotechology,
- desertification,
- hazardous wastes,
- land management,
- mountains,
- oceans and coastal zones,
- radioactive wastes,
- solid wastes and sewage,
- toxic chemicals,
- water-resources.

The UK Government adopted the framework during the 1992 UN Rio de Janeiro Earth Summit.

BACKWATERS - An old channel of a meandering watercourse that still remains connected to it.

BEST VALUE - The Best Value Act (Local Government Act 1999) put a duty on local authorities to make arrangements to secure the continuous improvement in the way their functions are exercised, and to have regard for a combination of economy, efficiency and effectiveness. All functions of a local authority must be fundamentally reviewed in relation to the four Cs of Compare, Challenge, Compete and Consult within a five year period.

BIODIVERSITY - The variation and number of different living components in an environment including their genetic diversity. The larger the number of species and individuals of one species the larger the gene pool, which ultimately will benefit the ecosystem. In the context of rivers and burns this could be applied to all the living elements within, outside and around these aquatic areas.

BIOCHEMISTRY - The chemical nature of living things. More specifically it is the study of the chemical components that compose the basic make-up for all living things and the reactions and interactions which occur within the organisms body.

BROWNFIELD SITE - Previously developed land. Brownfield sites are often thought to be contaminated; in fact the majority are entirely free from contamination and may provide havens for a wide variety of valuable wildlife species.

CARR HABITATS - Fen vegetation (see below) with trees.

CATCHMENT - The total area of land from which water drains into any given river or reservoir.

CATCHMENT MANAGEMENT - managing the entire drainage area - with the aim of ensuring water is available for different uses, eg irrigation, supply, and minimising erosion and pollution, and to minimise flooding.

COMBINED SEWER - A drainage system taking both waste water from properties and surface water arising from road run-off (Effluent is then taken away to the local Waste Water Treatment Works for treatment).

COMBINED SEWER OVERFLOW - an emergency overflow arrangement from the sewer to the local stream or river, found in areas which are served by a combined sewer. Designed to operate during extreme rainfall events when rain water enters the system and overloads the system. Rather than in a back up of effluent in the drains, the result is a discharge of diluted effluent into the local watercourse.

CULVERT - A covered channel or pipe, which completely encompasses a river or a burn.

ECOLOGY - The scientific study of the interactions between the living components and their environment, with attention to the biological and physical factors, and the external and internal relations.

ECOSYSTEM - A biological community and the physical environment associated with it.

FEN HABITATS - The vegetation that grows on naturally waterlogged land and eventually forms peat.

FLASH FLOODS - in areas with rapidly draining surfaces heavy rainfall can cause the flow in watercourses to rise very quickly and suddenly, sometimes sending a wall of water downstream. The force of the flow can cause damage and carry debris, which may result in blockage and flooding. Urbanisation and positive piped drainage systems increase the risk of flash floods; Sustainable Urban Drainage Systems reduce the risk.

FLUVIAL - Of streams and rivers.

GABIONS - The rectangular steel mesh structures used to build free-draining retaining walls. They are usually basket shaped and filled with rocks.

GEOMORPHOLOGY - The study of the evolution of landforms and the processes involved.

GEOTEXTILE - A strong durable, non-biodegradable sheet of woven plastic, used to reinforce soil, banks, and footpaths.

GREENFIELD SITE - undeveloped land, but maybe intensive agriculture.

GREENSPACE - An area set aside for the protection and enjoyment of nature.

HABITAT - A place where an organism lives.

HYDROLOGY - The study of all forms of water (rain, snow, ice, water) on the earth's surface.

HYDROGEOMORPHOLOGY - The study of the influence of water on of land, and the processes involved.

LADES - (or Leat) an artificial channel diverting water from a burn or river to provide a supply of sufficient height to drive a water wheel.

LANDFILL TAX FUNDING - Use of the levy payable on waste going to landfill for environmentally beneficial works within 10 miles of a landfill site.

LOCAL AGENDA 21 - The application of the Agenda 21 framework at a local level. All local authorities are required to have Agenda 21 Plans.

MARGIN(AL) - The area near the border or bank.

MEANDERS - see diagram

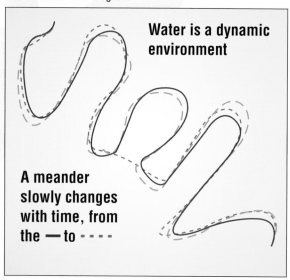

Water is a dynamic environment

A meander slowly changes with time, from the — to - - - -

METEOROLOGY - The study of the influence of the earth's atmosphere on the climate and weather patterns.

MILLPONDS - collected water used for powering water mills.

MONASTIC FISHPONDS - Fishponds built by monks to provide a source of food.

PHYSIOCHEMISTRY - The relationship between chemistry and the physical nature of the subject.

POINT BARS - sediment deposits on the inside of meanders.

POINT SOURCE DISCHARGES - eg sewage and industrial effluents. Discharges that are released into the watercourse at specific points. The opposite is diffuse pollution, consisting mainly of runoff from urban areas and farm land.

RIFFLES & POOLS -see diagram

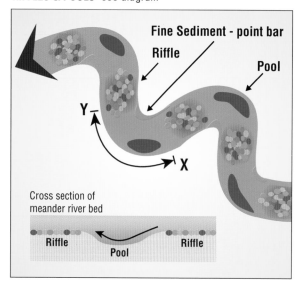

Fine Sediment - point bar
Riffle
Pool
Y
X
Cross section of meander river bed
Riffle
Pool
Riffle

RIPARIAN - The banks of a stream, or river.

RIPARIAN OWNER - the owner of the bank and watercourse bed.

SILTATION - where the material being carried downstream reaches a stretch of slower flowing water and settles out on the bed of the watercourse.

SEPARATE DRAINAGE SYSTEM - Foul effluent is taken away by one network of pipes to be treated. A separate system is used for rain water routing to the nearest burn or river. Cross-connections, the incorrect connection of foul drains to the surface water system, can cause pollution of watercourses. They can arise when downstairs toilets are added to a property during extension work, or from washing machines, when both are incorrectly plumbed in to the surface water pipework. Effluent intended to enter the foul drainage system, ends up in a watercourse.

STORM FLOWS - during storm conditions the amount of rainfall increases considerably, and the average is way surpassed, hence the term.

SWALE - A very shallow grass channel maintained by mowing, which provides a route for surface water. The swales slow the flow and help reduce pollution; they also provide some storage capacity which helps reduce the risk of flooding downstream. Often connected to detention or retention features such as basins, ponds and wetlands for storage and treatment of surface water prior to its discharge to adjacent watercourse.

TAIL RACE - an artificial channel dug downstream of a watermill to increase the height of the fall of water, and hence obtain more power for use in the mill.

TOXIC COMPONENTS AND HEAVY METALS - Potentially toxic metals that are used in various industrial processes. The common ones are copper, lead, zinc, cadmium and chromium.

WEIR - A wall built across the river, to raise the water level upstream, sometimes for a mill, sometimes for navigation purposes on canalised rivers, sometimes used to control irrigation. Weirs can block the movement of fish.

WHARVE OR WHARF - A berth situated parallel to the waterfront. It can be either a solid or open structure, depending on its use.

Acknowledgements

This report has been the work of over 80 different individuals who have willingly shared their enthusiasm and experience. Especial thanks to the following people:

Task Group and main contributors
Frank Guz, Dundee City Council, Chair;
Katherine Bradshaw, Brian D'Arcy, Ian Fox, Stephanie Harrison, Malcom MacConnachie, Neil McLean, David McNay SEPA; David Jamieson, Bob McCafferty, The City of Edinburgh Council; Nigel Holmes, River Restoration Centre; Katherine Leys, SNH; Peter Pollard, SWT; Elizabeth Leighton, WWF; Chris Soulsby, University of Aberdeen.

Urban Design Alliance Working Group
John Bircumshaw, Institution of Civil Engineers, Chair;
Mary Brookes, Moore, Piet and Brooke, Landscape Institute; John Turner, Leeds City Council; Jean Venables, Crane Environmental; Robert Huxford, Institution of Civil Engineers.

CIWEM Workshop Contributors
Bill Ashcroft, Aberdeen Council; Lachlan Cowan, Babtie Group; Stewart McMillan, Carl Bro; Mike Hetherington, City of Edinburgh Council; Gilbert Fraser, ESW; Ian Ludbrook, Falkirk Council; Alistair Moir; Maclolm Wilson, Fife Council; Dr Fiona Becker, Halcrow Crouch; Martin Dean, Nichol Slaven, North Lanarkshire Council; June Dawson, Rod Wallace, SEPA; Tim Dixon, Stirling Council; Neil Campbell, Sir Frederick Snow and Partners; Luan Anderson, WA Fairhurst; Steven Bell, WWF.

Scoping Study Workshop Contributors
Marc Becker, Jenni Brown, Sean Caswell, Alan Church, Paul Copestake, Linda Davis, Mike Devlin, Marie Donald, Mark Eggeling, Ian Fozzard, Sarah Gilman, Nigel Goody, David Harley, Scot Mathieson, David McNay, Ruth Rush, Huw Thomas, SEPA; Ken Dougan, Glasgow City Council; Angela Wiseman, Scottish Executive; Eliane Reid, Nicky Wood, SNH; Karen Haywood, West Lothian Council; Steve Young, Young Associates.

Other Contributions and Consultees (not already included above)
Andrew Wallace, Association of Salmon Fisheries Boards; Annie O'kane, CSCT Central Scotland; Chris Dyson; Ross Gardiner, Fresh Water Fisheries Lab; David Crichton, CGU Insurance; Brian Reed, CIRIA; John Crawford, East Ayrshire Council; Dave Gorman, Falkirk Council; Alastair D Young, Judith Parsons, Glasgow City Council; Jock Maxwell, Adrian Watkins, Meedhurst Project Management; Jenny Fausset, Midlothian Council; Gary Templeton, The Moray Council; Martyn McKeown, North Ayrshire Council; I G Lawson, North Lanarkshire Council; Jane Wright, Scottish Anglers National Association; David Howell, Willie Duncan, Scottish Natural Heritage; Drew Aitken, Peter Campbell, Willie Halcrow (Director, East Region), Julie Holmes, Jennifer Learmonth, Gaye McKissock, Kiri Walker, Sheila Winstone, SEPA; David Dunkley, Scottish Executive; Dr John Sheldon, West Lothian Council.

Edited by Robert Huxford and Helen Taylor, Institution of Civil Engineers. Honorary editor and project managed by Katherine Bradshaw, on behalf of the Habitat Enhancement Initiative Project Board, SEPA.